Creating Social Value

CREATING SOCIAL VALUE

A GUIDE FOR LEADERS AND CHANGE MAKERS

Cheryl Kiser and Deborah Leipziger
with J. Janelle Shubert

Routledge
Taylor & Francis Group
LONDON AND NEW YORK

First publishing 2014 by Greenleaf Publishing Limited

Published 2017 by Routledge
2 Park Square, Milton Park, Abingdon, Oxon OX14 4RN
711 Third Avenue, New York, NY 10017, USA

Routledge is an imprint of the Taylor & Francis Group, an informa business

Copyright © 2014 Babson College

Cover by LaliAbril.com

British Library Cataloguing in Publication Data:
A catalogue record for this book is available from the British Library.

ISBN-13: 978-1-906093-99-0 (pbk)
ISBN-13: 978-1-907643-97-2 (hbk)

≈

This book is dedicated to the Babson students who joined our journey, and to Entrepreneurial Leaders and Change Makers of all kinds everywhere.

≈

~

With Gratitude

We are grateful to Toyota Motor Corporation for its generous support of the founding of The Babson Social Innovation Lab. Toyota's influence not only gave us the opportunity to chronicle our students' journey to understand how to create economic and social value simultaneously, but also allows our students to be exposed to the Toyota Production System as a more sustainable and efficient design for achieving both.

We are grateful to Alan and Harriet Lewis for their generosity and vision to found The Lewis Institute for Social Innovation. Their leadership exemplifies the courage required by business leaders and entrepreneurs who are committed to creating both economic and social value everywhere.

~

Contents

Foreword

The world needs a new kind of business leader. A leader "able to make ethical decisions in the face of strategic unknowns, serve the environment and society while also serving the needs of investors and shareholders and understand how their personality and the social context in which they operate impacts their leadership."[1]

Here at Babson we intentionally develop leaders who will be skilled at creating economic and social value simultaneously and not sequentially.

The role of business in society has shifted dramatically and now more is expected in ways that the business world never anticipated. It is essential that the business leaders we educate know how to create social value as skillfully as they create economic value.

I want to thank the students from our MBA course, *Social Value Creation Matters*, and the companies they interviewed, for sharing their insights. We asked our students to take a journey and interview company executives in such a way that the insights they gained would

1 Greenberg, D., K. McKone-Sweet and H.J. Wilson (2011) *The New Entrepreneurial Leader: Developing Leaders Who Shape Social and Economic Opportunity* (San Francisco: Berrett-Koehler Publishers).

be real and relevant to helping them better understand how to create social value, no matter what role they take on. This was not a course in corporate social responsibility (CSR). Rather, it was a course in corporate social relevance. Whether inside of large organizations, venture start-ups, government organizations, or NGOs, being aware of what one needs to know, what one needs to do, and who one needs to be to drive both economic value and social value is the most relevant thing we can do to address and advance the *new* role of business in society.

Dennis Hanno
Provost and Senior Vice President
Babson College

Acknowledgments

Thank you to Len Schlesinger, President Emeritus of Babson College and the Baker Foundation Professor at Harvard Business School. This book took form as a result of his vision and influence in creating a world-class business school that educates leaders who create economic and social value simultaneously, not sequentially; and shapes leaders who will reshape the world.

This book was born of a strong desire and passion to share with the reader the insights gained by engaging with students, business leaders, faculty, and entrepreneurs of all kinds to better understand how social value is created inside both large companies and small start-ups. We knew it would be an adventure driven by the students in our class. We wanted their perspectives and inquiry to be real and relevant, not hypothetical, and based on a generous sharing of ideas between themselves and the courageous souls on the front line.

Many thanks and gratitude go to:

Jan Shubert, partner, co-creator, and scholar extraordinaire.

Deborah Leipziger, partner, co-author, lexicographer, translator of ideas, synthesizer of thoughts, and passionate soul who understands the complexities of living at the intersection of business and society.

Emily Weiner, impeccable editor, incredible partner, producer and creator of memorable experiences, and fellow inhabitant of the unpredictable and often unknowable landscape that we navigate every day at The Lewis Institute and Babson Social Innovation Lab.

Lindsey Tarr, superhero of the visual realm who, for two years, took our words and drew images and created pictures that would help others better understand what Social Value Creation looks like.

From Day One, Dennis Hanno supported, inspired, and provided pathways for many of us to take action to make a significant difference in the world. Supporting the course that this book is based on is one example.

Nan Langowitz for belief in our work, encouragement, direction and support for a not-so-usual business course charting an important journey for our students and Babson College.

Danna Greenberg, Kate McKone-Sweet, and H. James Wilson whose work helped our students assess their own potential to become New Entrepreneurial Leaders, and provided a framework and logic to better understand the extraordinary people profiled in this book.

Ana-Lisa Jones for being an exceptional Lewis Institute Fellow and working to make this book a reality with her interviews, writing, and editing.

Karene Alexander-Thorne for her dedication and curiosity in assisting our class and journey.

To our students who, in being curious seekers, were able to see the potential impact of this journey.

Fall 2011 Class

Andrew Helming, Ariana Zadek, Beatrice Semexant, Brooke Carter, David Brown, Dennis Lui, Eric Felz, Ethan Carlson, George Pararas-Carayannis, Johan de Borst, Jonathan Chuang, Jordan Gilbert, Justin DeMello, Kelly Murphy, Matthew Follett, Neralee Patel, Rosa

Slegers, Ryan Fuller, Ryan Wright, Scott Kirker, Shelly Goehring, and Vilomi Patel.

Fall 2012 Class

Adam Carmichael, Andrew Starr, Bo-Huei Lin, Courtney Farrell, George Lambert, Hillary Mann, Jennifer Cashton, John Sundborg, Joseph Plummer, Kate Mills, Kellie Chung, Krista Buckland Reisner, Lauren O'Gorman, Matthew Belkin, Michael Miller, Michael Sullivan, Mikaela Callahan, Mir Ahmad, Nick DiMatteo, Nicole Needham, Nisha Bhinde, Nusrath Khan, Paul DiSarcina, Rebecca Brown, Ross Hanson, and Sindhu Suresh.

To our generous business leaders and entrepreneurs who shared the experiences of their personal and professional journey in leading and creating social value for their organizations:

Jon Carson, BiddingForGood
Dave Stangis, Campbell Soup Company
John Viera, Ford Motor Company
David Berdish, Ford Motor Company
Mike Brady, Greyston Bakery
Ariel Hauptman, Greyston Bakery
Kevin Thompson, IBM
Eric Hudson, Preserve
Shainoor Khoja, Roshan
Rachel Weeks, School House
Shawn Gensch, Target
Nate Garvis, Founder of Naked Civics, formerly of Target
Lynnette McIntire, UPS
Rose Stuckey Kirk, Verizon
Kathy Brown, Verizon
Chris Lloyd, Verizon

Many thanks to Claire Jackson, John Stuart, and Dean Bargh at Greenleaf Publishing for their interest, support, and enthusiasm for our work; and to our editor Jenny Congrave.

Cheryl Kiser, Executive Director, The Lewis Institute and
Babson Social Innovation Lab

An introduction to creating social value

"In Babson's best tradition of bringing together Entrepreneurs of All Kinds™ to create sustainable economic and social value, Creating Social Value marshals substantial new insights and thought leadership for social innovators."

Kerry Healey, President, Babson College

"Innovation is active, not reactive; creative, not routinized; and aimed at breakthroughs, not incremental change."

Philip Mirvis, Bradley Googins, and Cheryl Kiser,
Corporate Social Innovation

Creating social value is a journey for which each company charts its own path through unknowable and complex terrain. The entrepreneurial leaders profiled in this book are trailblazers, using strategy and innovation to generate profits and social value simultaneously, not sequentially. In the words of Campbell Soup Company CEO

Denise Morrison: "profit and social value are part of the DNA of our company; a double helix, inextricably linked."[1]

This book allows the reader to accompany these entrepreneurial leaders on their journey. It shows them taking action amid uncertainty; activating change within their companies, their sectors, and their value chains; and even co-creating partnerships with their competitors.

Social innovation is about the use of language. While writing this book, we realized that the leaders we profiled use language in intentional ways to activate social value outcomes. By using seemingly common terms and phrases, these leaders were able to re-orient the mindset of individual influencers and their organization and, as a result, change the social and environmental outcomes and direction of the company. Leaders like Dave Stangis from Campbell Soup Company use language to activate social innovation both internally and externally. By adopting the term "destination goals," Dave created a context for new behavior, leading his colleagues to adopt a broader time horizon in which social innovation could be promoted and nurtured. Language is a powerful tool and new words do not necessarily have to be created to signal a shift. Rather, using existing words and phrases in new contexts can be a significant motivator and activator of change because this new language taps into something beyond our cognitive understanding and touches a higher set of values. Throughout this book, we have bolded some of these important change words and phrases.

The following examples of social value creation are profiled in this book:

Dave Stangis of Campbell Soup Company has created **destination goals** to describe the long-term vision of the company to nourish its customers, employees, and neighbors. The term "**destination goals**" also signals the long view of social value creation and its potential to and inspire an entire company. Often goals simply re-create the past or predict the future. **Destination goals** take the company outside of

1 Denise Morrison, CEO of Campbell Soup Company, Presentation at Boston College Center for Corporate Citizenship, April 21, 2013.

the confines of the past by allowing them to reimagine and redesign a different future.

Roshan has worked on **nation-building**, creating physical infrastructure in Afghanistan, a country decimated by war. The company is hiring local women who usually remain in the home. By creating mobile banking, Roshan has empowered the population and fought corruption.

Ford is redefining its mission, imagining a different future in which it provides mobility solutions, rather than only manufacturing cars. Ford is working with Toyota to **co-create** technologies to combat climate change.

School House has brought garment manufacturing back to North Carolina from Asia, **on-shoring** production in ways that allow for higher quality products and the re-emergence of the textile industry in Durham, North Carolina.

Eric Hudson founded Preserve with an understanding of the **mutual influence** of companies, developing partnerships to source raw materials from recycled materials, such as with Stonyfield from which he sources plastic; and designs innovative products which are fully recycled and recyclable.

Greyston Bakery has developed **Open-hiring** and **PathMaking** to combat poverty in Southwest Yonkers, New York.

Target is working to transform and redesign the retail experience. **Shared media** has allowed Target to communicate in new ways with its customers and associates.

Verizon, through **Shared Success**, is creating new services to promote access to healthcare through telemedicine and by providing technologies that make buildings more energy-efficient.

IBM's program is an example of a new reality in which the roles of government and the private sector blur to develop new mechanisms for collaboration. This is what Kevin Thompson of IBM calls **sector blur**.

BiddingForGood has developed a new market for helping non-profits to fundraise by using auctions.

UPS has worked to understand its impact on the planet, building a **materiality matrix** of the issues that matter to its stakeholders, while working to create a culture which fosters social innovation.

This book also is an entrepreneurial endeavor. Cheryl Kiser, Executive Director of The Lewis Institute and Babson Social Innovation Lab, wanted to create a unique educational experience that would bring executives from large and small companies into the MBA classroom. Cheryl brought together the people she knew from her years of working with leaders in the field of Corporate Social Responsibility. Using her network to curate a real and relevant classroom experience, the students would not simply be observers. Rather, they would engage directly with the executives and entrepreneurs, drafting their ideas which became the raw material for this book. Cheryl started by tapping into who she was, who she knew, and what she knew, then used the resources she had at hand to design a graduate-level course. This book is the result of her vision to capture content from the interactions between students and business leaders, and create a roadmap that demonstrates how to create social value within different contexts.

The companies profiled in this book are moving towards becoming **generative**[2] rather than extractive. In a **generative** economy, companies need to address and grapple with social problems. Being **generative** allows companies to be relevant and to engage with customers and employees in new ways, addressing unmet needs and tapping into markets for new products and services.

A Social Value Creation Manifesto

Social value creation is about co-creation

Companies do not create social value in a vacuum. To use the language of Tata, the Indian conglomerate, companies **co-create** social value. Unlocking social value is a process of co-creation between society, stakeholders, and company leadership. Companies can create social value by considering the economic, environmental, and social aspects of their impact as well as how to increase well-being and development.

Social value creation is about design

Social innovators need design to implement their vision—whether it is a new product, a new business, or a shift in their sourcing policies and practices. Ford is manufacturing its cars from green materials and making them more fuel-efficient. Target has redesigned how it sells certain products in order to prevent crime and drug abuse.

---

2 The authors are grateful to Marjorie Kelly, a Fellow at the Tellus Institute for coining the term "generative." See Marjorie Kelly (2012), *Owning Our Future: The Emerging Ownership Revolution, Journeys to a Generative Economy* (San Francisco: Berrett-Koehler).

Social value creation is about accessibility

Social innovators find ways of bringing the disenfranchised into the business model. Verizon has done this by making mobile devices accessible to people with disabilities. Roshan brought women into its workforce in Afghanistan, where few women are employed outside of the home.

Social value creation is about leveraging business to address social issues

From obesity to corruption to road safety, the companies featured in this book are using social problems as a starting point for new products and new businesses.

Social value creation is about transformation

Whether companies are involved in **nation-building** or changing the sector or the community they operate in, social value creation is about deep, long-term change, not just cosmetic changes.

Social value creation is about developing infrastructure

In order to enter new markets, companies may need to develop the necessary infrastructure. In Afghanistan, Roshan promoted infrastructure around health and water, and assisted with the construction of airports.

Social value creation requires training

Whether it is to raise awareness within a sector, or to prepare employees, social value creation requires extensive training to allow for change. Nearly all of the companies profiled in this book invest in training. For example, Verizon, Greyston Bakery, and IBM demonstrate the need to invest in employees.

Social value creation is about reimagining the purpose of business

To create social value, a company may need to reimagine its purpose and structure. Ford now sees itself as a company providing mobility solutions rather than as just a car manufacturer. School House has begun to source its production line in the U.S. rather than in Asia. It may be necessary to reimagine the business model, to create lasting social value.

Mechanisms for creating social value

Companies can create social value through several mechanisms, including social innovation, social entrepreneurship, policies, products, services, collaboration, and core competencies.

Social Innovation

The companies profiled in this book are innovators, co-creating forms of social innovation that change the way they do business, whether it is:

The development of new products and sourcing of raw materials:	Preserve
Innovative ways of hiring:	Greyston Bakery
Products that address unmet social needs:	Verizon
Creating new forms of leadership development:	IBM
Creating new markets for fundraising:	BiddingForGood
Nation-building:	Roshan
On-shoring:	School House
Partnering with a competitor:	Ford
New channels of communication:	Target
New products and systems:	Campbell Soup Company
Sustainability systems:	UPS

Definition

Corporate Social Innovation is a strategy that combines a unique set of corporate assets (innovation capacities, marketing skills, managerial acumen, employee engagement, scale, etc.) in collaboration with the assets of other sectors to **co-create** breakthrough solutions to complex economic, social, and environmental issues that impact the sustainability of both business and society.

Social innovation differs from corporate responsibility in significant ways. It is strategic and it leverages a wide range of corporate assets and core competencies.

What makes Social Innovation different?

Source: Jason Saul, author of *Social Innovation, Inc.: Five Strategies for Driving Business Value through Social Change* and CEO of Mission Measurement

Traditional CSR	Social Innovation
Philanthropic intent	Strategic intent
Money, manpower	R&D, corporate assets
Employee volunteerism	Employee development
Contracted service providers	NGO/government partners
Social and eco-services	Social and eco-innovations
Social good	Sustainable social change

What are the drivers of social innovation?

There are many drivers that can promote social innovation. Many of the companies profiled in this book start with a global challenge as a point of departure. Combating poverty is a challenge that Greyston Bakery addresses in its **open-hiring**. For Verizon, Campbell Soup Company, IBM, and BiddingForGood, business opportunities drive social innovation and vice versa. In other instances, leaders within the company, such as Lynnette McIntire at UPS, use employee engagement as a driver of social innovation. New partnership possibilities have also helped to promote social innovation at Preserve, Greyston Bakery, and Ford.

6 Drivers of CSI

Source: Mirvis, Googins, and Kiser 2012

Social Enterprise

Several of the companies profiled in this book are social enterprises. Examples include Greyston Bakery, Preserve, and School House as they have a social mission built into their business model. School House is building a line of "fair fashion" and Greyston Bakery is combating poverty by baking brownies to hire people.

Many of the executives we profile in this book are social entrepreneurs or **entrepreneurs inside**. A social entrepreneur is an individual:

- "Adopting a mission to create and sustain social value (not just private value);

- Recognizing and relentlessly pursuing new opportunities to serve that mission;

- Engaging in a process of continuous innovation, adaptation, and learning;

- Acting boldly without being limited by resources currently in hand;

- Exhibiting heightened accountability to the constituencies served and for the outcomes created."[3]

Even without working in a social enterprise, the business leaders profiled in this book could be considered **entrepreneurs inside**.

Definition

Entrepreneurs inside include a combination of people, resources, and structures that create the ecosystem inside the company. Just as entrepreneurs see business opportunities, entrepreneurs inside see ways to create social value and financial value. Examples of entrepreneurial ventures range from: "the development of a new market-making innovation, product, service, or program...; to the creation of an entrepreneurial culture within their organization or community... to catalyzing change across a networked infrastructure (e.g., addressing food deserts through public-private community networks.)"[4]

Entrepreneurial Thought and Action® and the New Entrepreneurial Leader

Babson invented the methodology for entrepreneurship education nearly a century ago and has been convening, leading, and advancing Entrepreneurial Thought and Action® as the most positive force on the planet for the creation of sustainable economic and social value. Babson's mission is to develop what it defines as the "New Entrepreneurial Leaders."

Entrepreneurial leadership is inspired by, but is separate from, entrepreneurship. It is a leadership approach that can be applied in

---

3 Dees, J.G. (2011) 'The Meaning of "Social Entrepreneurship",' Center for the Advancement of Social Entrepreneurship, www.caseatduke.org/documents/dees_sedef.pdf.
4 Babson Entrepreneurs Experience Lab, Experiences of Entrepreneurs Inside, 2013, www.elab.businessinnovationfactory.com/elements/experiences-entrepreneurs-inside/research-methodology

any organization, not just start-ups. The new entrepreneurial leader embraces three principles that add up to nothing less than a fundamentally new world-view of business and a new logic of decision-making.

With a world characterized by rapid change and increasing uncertainty, leaders are required to be **cognitively ambidextrous**, able to shift between traditional "prediction logic" (choosing actions based on analysis of known trends) and "creation logic" (taking action despite considerable unknowns). Guiding this different way of thinking and acting, is a different world-view of business and society, where the simultaneous creation of social, environmental, and economic value is the order of the day. Entrepreneurial leaders also leverage their understanding of themselves and their social context to guide effective action.

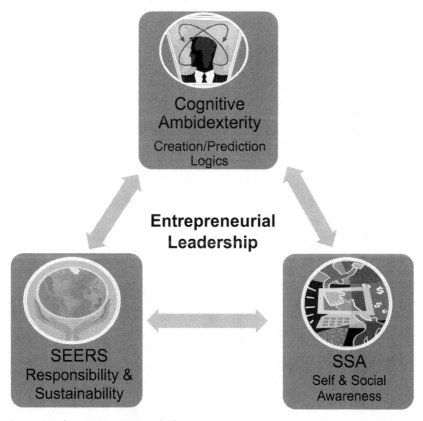

Source: Greenberg, McKone-Sweet, and Wilson 2012

The creation of this book has been an example of Entrepreneurial Thought and Action® and it identified entrepreneurial leaders as guides in the process of discovering how social value is created. The course, Social Value Creation Matters, with regard to how it was conceived, developed, and delivered, as well as with whom we engaged, was an example of using who we are, what we know, who we know, and available resources to create an experiential journey into the realm of social value creation.

For much of their careers, the authors have been working with some of the world's most successful companies and impressive individuals who occupy the most senior ranks of their organizations, driving social value creation through programs and initiatives that benefit their organizations and society. The authors noticed that many of the attributes of individuals who drove some of the best corporate citizenship/CSR programs/social innovation were the attributes of a new kind of entrepreneurial leader.

This book is about this new kind of leader and the sweet spot of social value creation. It is about the students and their intellectual journey to better understand the very ambiguous and complex notion of social value creation. It is about who, how, and what it took to actually get started and make the kind of business and social impact that so many strive to achieve. Our students interviewing the people in this book were very interested in the thinking and acting of the entrepreneurial leaders, and how they were able to create social impact. The following is a set of questions that we sought to answer from the point of view of the individuals we interviewed:

- Who am I (my identity as shaped by culture, context, skills, and abilities)?

- What do I know (my knowledge and training)?

- Whom do I know (my professional and social network)?

- How do I bring together these three elements into a network of participants who can **co-create** an opportunity?

Most of today's organizations were built *through* entrepreneurship but ironically are not built *for* entrepreneurship. Many entrepreneurial leaders spend intense amounts of time learning what it takes to get something unpredictable done in an inherently bureaucratic, often non-supportive, prediction-driven environment. **Entrepreneurs inside** have the capacity to change organizational behavior from within. They are the harbingers of what organizations need to think about and become in the very near future, if not now.[5]

Sources

The Business Innovation Factory: www.businessinnovationfactory.com.

Greenberg, D., K. McKone-Sweet, and H.J. Wilson (2012) *The New Entrepreneurial Leader* (San Francisco: Berrett-Koehler).

Kiser, C. (2010) 'Intrapreneurial Behavior and eBay's Robert Chatwani', U.S. Chamber of Commerce Foundation, bclc.uschamber.com/blog/2010-03-22/intrapreneurial-behavior-and-ebay%E2%80%99s-robert-chatwani-1-2-0, accessed March 22, 2010.

Kiser, C. (2010) 'Intrapreneurial Behavior and Robert's Rules', US Chamber of Commerce Foundation, bclc.uschamber.com/blog/2010-03-24/intrapreneurial-behavior-and-roberts-rules-2-2, accessed March 24, 2010.

Mirvis P., B. Googins, and C. Kiser (2012) 'Corporate Social Innovation', unpublished article.

5 Greenberg, D., K. McKone-Sweet and H.J. Wilson (2012) *The New Entrepreneurial Leader* (San Francisco: Berrett-Koehler).

1
Strategy and innovation

How does one of the best-known food companies work to promote a healthier range of products? How can a company known for its iconic brand work within the urban community in which it is headquartered to reduce hunger and obesity? Campbell Soup Company shows how a company can articulate **destination goals** to create social value for its consumers, its employees, communities, and the natural environment through innovation.

This chapter is based on classroom discussions and interviews from 2011 and 2012, and does not represent a totality of the activities in which the company is engaged. The diagram at the beginning of the chapter is meant to orient the reader as to the contents of the chapter rather than the breadth of issues covered by the company.

Campbell Soup Company

"There is an enormous space here for innovation to generate a competitive advantage to industries that are able to get ahead of the game in developing foods and beverages that taste good and are healthful."

Dr. Julio Frenk, Dean of Harvard School of Public Health[1]

1 Miller, T. (2011) "Can food industry, governments work together to fight obesity?" PBS Newshour, The Rundown, A Blog of News and Insight, www.pbs.org/newshour/rundown/2011/09/can-food-industry-governments-work-together-to-fight-obesity.html, September 20, 2011.

Background

Campbell Soup Company is a 140-year-old company which manufactures and markets convenience food products under its own brand. The company features a diversified product line across five divisions: U.S. Simple Meals, North American Food Service, International Simple Meals & Beverages, U.S. Beverages, and Global Baking & Snacking. The product line is sold worldwide and includes the iconic soups, as well as canned pasta, beans, gravy, juices, beverages, and baked goods and snacks. Popular products like Goldfish Crackers, Pepperidge Farm Bread, Pace Salsa, Prego pasta sauce, Spaghetti-Os, and Swanson Stock are all Campbell's products.

In the United States, Canada, and Latin America, the company's products are resold to consumers in retail food chains and other retail, commercial, and non-commercial establishments. Over the fiscal year ending July 2012, Campbell's had $7.7 billion in net sales, $1.3 billion in earnings before interest and taxes (EBIT), and $846 million in net earnings. Campbell's currently employs over 19,000 people across 20 countries and 31 plant sites.

Corporate social responsibility (CSR) and sustainability at Campbell's

CSR at Campbell Soup Company is aligned with the company's strategic growth initiatives. The company's growth strategy can be summarized as the pursuit of three strategic objectives:

- **To become a more innovative company,** by being "critically focused on consumer-driven innovation in products and packaging as the primary driver of organic growth"

- **To become a more balanced company,** in an effort to "drive our company's growth by providing a wide array of delicious, nutritious, and convenient products across a growing global consumer base"

- **To become a more responsive company**, in order to "be far better positioned for engagement with new and growing consumer groups"[2]

Setting destination goals

Dave Stangis, Campbell Soup Company's Vice President of CSR and Sustainability, was instrumental in helping Campbell's to set **destination goals**. These ten-year goals are ambitious and set the company on a journey to create social value. Many companies set annual targets for CSR. According to Dave, "When you set annual targets, you think small: this is what we did this year; we think we can do that next year, let's make that our goal, and then if we're good we'll exceed it."[3] To Dave, short-term goals are more likely to be a description or a prediction.

Campbell's has established the following **destination goals** for 2020:

- **Nourishing Our Planet** by cutting the company's environmental footprint in half

- **Nourishing Our Consumers** by continually advancing the nutrition and wellness profile of the product portfolio

- **Nourishing Our Neighbors** by measurably improving the health of young people in our hometown community

- **Nourishing Our Employees** by promoting 100% employee engagement in CSR and sustainability[4]

---

2 *Ibid.*

3 Interview with Dave Stangis, "Using Creative Tension to Reach Big Goals," *MIT Sloan Management Review*, November 2011: 3.

4 *Ibid.*

Destination goals help to drive systems change, not just incremental change. By setting a destination, leaders within the company can then chart a course. **Destination goals** create a kind of creative tension; they inspire people to think in new ways and give employees permission to develop new types of design, whether it is packaging, manufacturing, or new sources of energy.

Dave is very candid about his view of what the **destination goals** should include:

> *I had advocated that one of our **destination goals** should be to feature the healthiest product portfolio on the planet. And I actually got buy-in from a number of our business leaders. But I didn't win over a couple businesses—and in the end, they were right. It was hard for these businesses to conceive of a strategy where the product portfolio can be the healthiest in the marketplace. We have created a strategy and direction around "choice." Making sure consumers can choose their version of what's best for them and their families across the portfolio.*
>
> *My goal is to put dedicated resources in each of the major business groups. These are resources I know the company needs, and I have worked and argued for this. We have made progress by placing a sustainability leader in procurement. The goal is the same in R&D and marketing.[5]*

Defining CSR and sustainability strategies at Campbell's

Campbell Soup Company has adopted a regimented approach toward including corporate social responsibility and sustainability in the core strategic planning for company growth and evolution. The company

5 Dave Stangis, Vice President for CSR and Sustainability, Campbell Soup Company, lecture at Babson, November 13, 2012.

conducts an annual strategic planning session for all company strategies, which includes corporate plans for CSR and sustainability programs. Campbell's considers CSR strategies as "core platforms that are incorporated into key business and functional-unit strategic plans with three-year time horizons and annual performance goals that then lead to executive and personal performance objectives."[6]

The strategic planning process for CSR at Campbell's includes a comprehensive assessment of the needs and desires of key internal and external stakeholders, as well as consideration for key trends in corporate social responsibility and sustainability within and between industries like their own. In short, Campbell's attempts to recognize and deliver upon as many areas of corporate focus as is economically and logistically possible to support the corporate mission statement of "Nourishing People's Lives Everywhere, Every Day." Their internal stakeholders range from C-suite executives down to functional-unit managers and contributors. The external stakeholders are too diverse to catalog, but they directly contribute to Campbell's CSR strategy via a range of engagements and an annual consumer survey.

In fact, the most recent Campbell's CSR consumer survey provided compelling input which helped to establish the need for Campbell's to provide special focus in the following four areas:

1. **Strategic community initiatives**: Giving back to the community is something that is expected. Food companies should also help minimize hunger in the community.

2. **Commitment to food safety**: A commitment to food safety should be listed as a priority for Campbell's in its CSR reporting to the public.

3. **Prioritizing affordability**: Manufacturing and marketing products in a way to keep food affordable, while maintaining

6 www.campbellsoupcompany.com/csr/pages/success/management-strategy-and-analysis.asp

shareowner value, should be included as a priority for the company.

4. **Championing nutrition:** Improving the nutritional content of food should also be a focus area, including a focus on using all-natural ingredients.[7]

Addressing hunger and obesity

Campbell Soup Company is headquartered in Camden, New Jersey, where hunger and obesity pose major challenges. Approximately 40% of Camden children aged 3–19 are obese.[8] Camden is also a food desert, with only one full-service grocery store.[9] Given the dire situation, the company is working to combat hunger and obesity in several innovative ways. Campbell's is the first food company to develop a metric to address obesity and hunger.

In order to meet its goal of "Nourishing our Neighbors," the company is working to turn its employees into social entrepreneurs. An example of how effectively the company has worked to catalyze its employees is the initiative "Just Peachy." One of Campbell's key partners in the community, the Food Bank of South Jersey, spoke to farmers to hear their concerns. One of the problems faced by peach farmers was the disposal of 800,000 pounds of peaches which were either too small or too blemished to sell. These peaches were delicious, but

---

7 www.campbellsoupcompany.com/csr/pages/success/stakeholder-engage ment.asp

8 United Way of New Jersey, www.uwccnj.org/work/uwcc_in_the_ community. For a full study on Camden, see: Rutgers Center for State Health Policy, New Jersey Childhood Obesity Survey, 2010; www .cshp.rutgers.edu/Downloads/8640.pdf.

9 Denise Morrison, CEO of Campbell Soup Company, Presentation at Boston College Center for Corporate Citizenship, April 21, 2013. Also New Jersey.com: www.nj.com/camden/index.ssf/2013/03/camden_to_ get_first_large_groc.html.

they just could not be sold in traditional venues. The peach farmers would spend $80,000–100,000 to dispose of the peaches, which was a waste of resources. The Food Bank of South Jersey had an idea: why not turn the blemished peaches into peach salsa? They didn't know if it was possible, or how to make it happen—but they knew a company that would know. Campbell's chefs developed the recipe and its employees canned 54,000 jars of peach salsa in hand-labeled jars in Campbell's facilities, using donated jars and cilantro. The initiative generated $100,000 for the Food Bank of South New Jersey which serves over 175,000 clients.

Campbell's is also addressing nutrition by creating healthier products. As part of Campbell's commitment to healthier foods that support healthier lifestyles, the company has achieved the following milestones in the U.S.:

- More than 300 products that are low in fat, saturated fat, and cholesterol

- More than 200 products with reduced levels of sodium (products launched at Food and Drug Administration (FDA) level of 480 mgs or reduced from original product by 10–50%)

- More than 200 products that have 100 calories or fewer per serving

- More than 75 products that are certified by the American Heart Association[10]

Long-term environmental goals

In addition to the remarkable progress and achievements of Campbell's CSR team since inception, the following long-term **destination goals** have been set, with a target to achieve them by 2020:[11]

10 *Ibid.*
11 Source of data: Dave Stangis, Vice President for CSR and Sustainability, Campbell Soup Company, presentation at Babson College, November 13, 2012.

- Reduce energy use by 35% and source 40% of energy from renewable or alternative energy sources

- Recycle 95% of waste generated globally

- Eliminate 100 million pounds of packaging from Campbell's products

- Make a positive impact on the lives of 100 million youth through volunteer, community, and signature programs

Since January 1, 2009, Campbell's:

- Now uses **1 billion fewer gallons of water** each year (a cumulative saving of more than 4.4 billion gallons)

- Now uses **450,000 fewer mmbtus** of energy each year (a cumulative saving of more than 280,000 metric tons of CO_2)

- Has initiated projects to extend its installed solar panels from a few kW to more than 12MW (8% of total energy)

- Has invested in projects that deliver cumulative **savings of more than $42.9 million**

In the 2012 fiscal year alone, Campbell's:

- Saved more than 11 million gallons of water and reduced greenhouse gas emissions by more than 83,000 metric tons of CO_2

- Saved more than 2.4 million pounds of packaging through package redesign and lightweighting

Figure 1.1 **Campbell's environmental and sustainability goals and dashboard**

Source: Campbell's 2013 performance update of the corporate social responsibility report[12]

2020 Environmental Sustainability Destination Goals

Primary
–   Cut the environmental footprint of our product portfolio in half (water and greenhouse gas [GHG] emissions/tonne product produced)*

Supporting
–   Reduce energy use by 35%, and source 40% of the electricity used from renewable or alternative energy sources
–   Recycle 95% of waste generated globally
–   Eliminate 100 million pounds of packaging from Campbell products
–   Deliver 100% of global packaging from sustainable materials (renewable, recyclable or from recycled content)
–   Reduce water use per lb. of ingredient by 20%
–   Reduce nitrogen applied per lb. of ingredient by 10%
–   Reduce GHGs per lb. of ingredient by 20%
*Relative reduction goals for energy use, water use and waste recycling in our operations are based on a baseline year of FY2008 performance.

12   www.campbellsoupcompany.com/csr/pages/planet/overview.asp#.UjLT 98bXbgt

Dave Stangis, Vice President, Public Affairs and Corporate Responsibility for Campbell Soup Company and President of the Campbell Soup Foundation

Dave Stangis joined the Campbell Soup Company team in September 2008 with responsibility for both designing and managing Campbell's CSR strategy and programs. He also oversees the Community Affairs strategy, including Campbell's signature Healthy Communities Initiative, as well as the activities of the Campbell Soup Foundation, the primary philanthropic arm of Campbell Soup Company.

Dave and his team work in collaboration with internal business units to deliver long-term business value across broad CSR platforms including the Marketplace, Community, Environmental Sustainability, and the Workplace. Since his arrival at Campbell's, the company has been named to the Dow Jones Sustainability Indices, *Corporate Responsibility Magazine*'s 100 Best Corporate Citizens List, and as one of the World's Most Ethical Companies by *Ethisphere Magazine*. He has made significant strides towards Campbell's CSR initiatives, with a focus on environmental sustainability.

Dave has over 20 years of experience in corporate social responsibility and the environment, health, and safety fields. He previously held the position of Global Director of Corporate Responsibility at Intel Corporation, where he developed and implemented Intel's CSR policies. His efforts helped Intel to achieve the top spot on the Dow Jones Sustainability Index for seven consecutive years. Dave is on the advisory boards of the Graham Sustainability Institute at the University of Michigan, Net Impact, University of Detroit College of Business, and *Ethical Corporation* magazine. In 2008, he was named one of the 100 Most Influential People in Business Ethics by *Ethisphere Magazine*. In 2011 and 2012, *Trust Across America* named Dave one of the Top 100 Thought Leaders in Trustworthy Business Behavior.

In addition to his CSR roles, Dave has a diverse résumé including experience in external affairs for Intel and in the field of environmental engineering for a number of firms in the earlier stages of his career. His educational background includes a BS degree from the University of Detroit, an MBA from the University of Michigan, and an MS in Occupational and Environmental Health from Wayne State University in Detroit.

From the viewpoint of Dave Stangis

'Opportunity and brand equity

Campbell's has more opportunities than other major U.S. food companies, and our potential is tremendous. Our portfolio provides us with a great opportunity to engage consumers. Our brand equity is significant and helped by the fact that we're one of the few food companies where the main brand is the same name as the company. Kraft is well-known for its Macaroni and Cheese and Nestlé is pretty close, but most people associate that brand with coffee or chocolate. We have a set of equities that, if we could change the dialogue and figure out how to take this warm, traditional, family brand value and turn that into the future of social impact, we would be successful. Basically, if we can change the way people look at food and health and what health and nutrition mean, we have a great opportunity.

'Consumer engagement strategy

We have some really interesting experiments going on around our social engagement. We have grown from zero capacity in digital to having a team of six within about a month's time frame. And, for the first time in my history with the company, we are considering the consumer engagement value of this initiative. Now we have the process and understanding in place. Our biggest opportunity is a consumer engagement strategy which we haven't fully amplified because very few consumers know about our current projects. Communication is a key challenge.

'Building a CSR team

I started by building my CSR team on my own with existing company resources. I created four charted teams, and I went to the leadership and asked to create a team around sustainability. They had HR, Workplace, Community, and Marketplace divisions. They had numbers, they had scope, and they planned how often to meet and what to meet about. In a consumer products organization, you can find a company organization that manages marketplace and consumer relationships, workplace, and community. These were already in place, so these were not needed as much as sustainability and a Sustainability Steering Committee. Yes, there were environmental people in the company, but this was not the same as building a sustainability team. Now, the sustainability team has been off to a great start and they behave almost like a board with a year-long agenda. They are organized; they know how to review the strategy. I have been with the company for four years and my job title has changed three times because the company is figuring out the value of this initiative.

I was hired as VP of Corporate Social Responsibility and Sustainability. There was actually a public affairs organization that dealt with the community and they were located in another part of the building. There was a management transition and Denise Morrison was appointed as our new CEO. She reorganized and brought community over to me. So, I went from having one part-time person working on CSR metrics and reporting, to now having a four- or five-person group of community affairs managers. There is someone that managed the volunteer program, general community affairs; the Campbell Soup Foundation came with that and a couple of support people. As the group grew, I was able to create a job for the part-time person. She found her passion in CSR, with no previous experience and has grown into the function well. We hired a sustainability analyst as well and are now up from five to seven people. We work as a small consulting group, making the strategic choice to grow from within. All group members have one year's experience in a formal CSR group, a few more if you count the years in the previous community/communications organization. This is all new to them and it has been tough as it requires performing at another level. But the trade-off is the opportunity to be entrepreneurial and creative. They can basically experiment with what they want, and my role is to act as a mentor and coach them along the way.

It is very difficult to assign accountability when strategies are shared between departments and diverse teams. There have been many examples of employees that get their hands dirty in the sustainability efforts, and then leave the company or position. This is a constant challenge in a competitive business where the business case isn't embraced by every manager. My work with our R&D organization is an example of this. We had a great individual that basically got pulled back into another part of the business. He loved doing the work, but his leadership didn't always see the value in the project. We are attempting to master both the process strategy and people strategy. The people that enter the program have a lot of passion, but when the people are gone, it goes back to a process strategy. We are there in some places such as packaging and design, and we are starting to get there in orientation and training. But there are a lot of places in the company where it is in the informal rather than formal processes through our people. Sometimes I win battles and sometimes I lose battles; and sometimes I find a talented person and then they leave the company. I'm not an empire builder who is running around saying "I need a six-person head count." Rather, I'm trying to demonstrate the value so that individuals see what's in it for them, no matter where they are in the company.

‘Social media

Social media is breaking down the traditional marketing barriers. Our company and all CPG [Consumer Packaged Goods] companies are made up of many brand managers who are all trained and perform in similar ways. Some of them love social media and want to dive in, and sometimes we lose them or sometimes we put them to work. A couple of years ago, we had this compelling cause-marketing program, not a CSR program, called "Help Grow Your Soup," which was all about helping individual consumers understand where their food comes from. From a consumer viewpoint, we were letting people know the authenticity of the products that we sell so that they can know the people who grew them. We brought school kids to urban farms all over the country and we did barn renovations that people could vote on. We got positive results that we could test the awareness and the affinity. But after one season, it was over because it was a one-year marketing agreement and then the next year we decided to do something else. Kraft then picked up a portion of it for the Triscuit brand, doubled it in size, and now is doing a great job with it.

It is helpful to think about these programs from a consumer engagement perspective and not a marketing perspective. CSR and sustainability do not run on the same cycle as a marketing campaign. There are four or five things that we are going to continually remind the consumer that we stand for, such as nutrition, young people, and health. A cool example out there now [fall of 2012] is a little experiment that our digital team and one of our integrated marketing teams inside the company wanted to do the first-of-its-kind Pinterest campaign that has to do with the green bean casserole. They are building the world's largest green bean casserole on Pinterest and every click gives a dollar to Feeding America. It reminds people of the Thanksgiving season and one of our products and partnerships. And it is also aligned with a non-profit partner that we have been working with for 20 years and will continue to work with for 20 years. It is a way to ladder up the story and not just some one-off marketing campaign. Rather than just focusing on incremental steps and campaigns, social media can help to reinforce everything we do as a company.

Questions from students for Dave Stangis, Vice President, Public Affairs and Corporate Responsibility for Campbell Soup Company and President of the Campbell Soup Foundation

Q: This question came to me when I was looking at your slide about the 24,000 solar panels supplying 15% of the energy for that plant. It seems like a lot of the CSR initiatives require large capital outlays and I was wondering if your board makes you stick to certain time frames where you realize a full return on those investments. It seems like something that must be difficult to measure so I wanted to see if this is something that they do and what that time frame may be.

A: Frankly, as hard as it is in the sustainability space, it is easier there than anywhere else. We try to keep the same ROI hurdle for capital projects in energy environments as we do with other ROI projects. Companies are not equipped today or there are very few people inside the company that have all the knowledge that they need to do renewable projects in a cost-effective way. You need tax people, you need legal people, you need energy people, and you need real estate people. There are all kinds of different groups involved. The renewable projects that we have been able to do are basically zero capital costs because we do not own these facilities but we agree to buy 100% of the power that they generate which provides the assurance to the operator that they can build. All of our renewable projects have been that way today.

The reason it is 15% in terms of power and not a bigger number is because what we have been able to do with the renewables is offset the coal or fuel oil or some other higher environmental impact energy source. But I do get asked because these projects are fairly complicated and even our board does not understand unless I explain them in detail. I am having dinner with one of the board members tomorrow night who asks me these questions all the time and she always wants to know how much we are investing, what the payback period is, and the toughest question to answer is whether this time and money could not be better invested in other projects.

At Intel, we set money aside for energy conservation projects, $4 million each year, so they only had to compete with other energy conservation projects which automatically took the ROI hurdle down. At Campbell's, we are looking at 20% ROI, but we may lower this if they really are in our sweet spot. It is not a formal policy but it is kind of agreed to for those of us who do the projects.

Q: We have read your biography and heard you talk about a part of your journey at Intel and a larger part of your journey at Campbell's. Can you help us see the point in your career where you said "man, this sustainability stuff can be pretty exciting?" What got you moving in that direction?

A: I can almost tell you the day! I spent 12 years at Intel. My background is in environment, health, and safety. I was hired at Intel in 1996 as a corporate safety engineer and I worked at an electric utility before that in Arizona as an environmental engineer. I wrote powered industrial truck policies and performed confined space and safety audits around the world, but somehow I must have been able to communicate complex topics in simple terms. After a year of being a safety engineer, Intel asked me to take a new role which, at the time, was called an environmental health and safety regulatory affairs manager. This was in 1998 and almost immediately Intel was faced with escalating campaigns from activists about chemicals in the plant and water and toxic chips. Within a week of the job there was a front-page story in *USA TODAY* that I still have today. Therefore, my job went from being a governmental affairs guy to a crisis manager. We had shareowner resolutions and communities asking tough questions and, all of a sudden, I was dealing with these external stakeholders in conflict resolution and understanding what they wanted. The other thing that happened in 1997 was the first movement towards standardized sustainability reporting for public companies, so these two things came together in the 1997–1998 time frame. I am working at a company with 85,000 people and $30 billion in revenue at the time; and even after I answered all those questions about community and environment they started asking about diversity, ethics, and compliance, and I was trying to package a cohesive response to what we were doing in this space. It was clear to me that we needed an organized function.

It took me two years of building the case and I still have some of the old slides. I went around and found out what other positions existed like this and got one person at a time aligned at Intel. After two years, I wore them out and they let me have the job, but they actually made me interview for it even after convincing them to create the position. Luckily, I got it and that was the point in time we created this function called Manager of Corporate Responsibility.

Q: I noticed that nutritional choices were one of your four pillars. I was wondering how you balance those choices with some of the non-nutritious choices that you may have out there and if you have a certain target for launching a certain number of products every year if a certain percentage has to be in that category or how you balance the negative products?

A: Not only is it a matter of balance but, in the U.S., we can clearly define what a nutritionally improved product is. We know what the positives are; and not just us, but the regulators know what the positives are, and if we increase those then we can communicate the benefits. If we take the negatives—the fats, the sodium, the sugars— and decrease those, then we can report that too. The FDA also has a definition of what constitutes a healthy product. In places where there are definitions that exist, we can draw those lines in the sand in our product portfolio and count and measure our improvement statistics.

We do not have a specific goal. The challenge for years had been that, if you talked to the CEO or some of the other business managers, you would hear that they felt they were singularly focused on sodium, but there is much more to the story. Improving nutrition or driving product reformulation is a challenge because sometimes we change the product to such an extent that it does not sell anymore. We have examples of products that were reformulated to be "better for you" that didn't sell well at all. You will not make people healthy by making a product that no one will eat. It has been a learning process and that is why the word "choice" is an explicit part of our strategy, and our goal is to be able to find and offer a healthy choice for every meal. Our Healthy Request® soups are one of the fastest-growing product lines that we have, but it does not work across the board.

We get challenged externally, but also by our major shareholders. They want to know what we are doing to change the eating behaviors of the world. Personally, I am a pessimist because I see the world moving from eating meals to snacking and grazing throughout the day. If you study demographics and sociology, it is possible to view the trends as disposable income increases and as people move from rural populations to urban populations; their nutritional habits do not improve. There are many areas we need to work on from public policy to food. The trend at Campbell's is that products have been getting healthier for the past several years, but I do not know how hard it is going to be to keep those numbers continuing to go in the right direction.

Sources

Interview with Dave Stangis, "Using Creative Tension to Reach Big Goals," *MIT Sloan Management Review*, November 2011.

Presentation by Dave Stangis, Campbell Soup Company, Babson, November 13, 2012.

Presentation by Denise Morrison, CEO, Campbell Soup Company, Boston College Center for Corporate Citizenship Conference, Boston, April 21, 2013.

2
Nation-building

How can a company address threats to the security of
its employees while fighting endemic corruption? How
can a telecommunications company work to rebuild a
war-torn country? Roshan is working to promote the
infrastructure of Afghanistan and creating social value
through nation-building. The company has revolutionized
the telecommunications and banking sectors while creating
opportunities for women in a country where female
employment is not the norm.

*This chapter is based on classroom discussions and interviews from
2011 and 2012, and does not represent a totality of the activities in
which the company is engaged. The diagram at the beginning of the
chapter is meant to orient the reader as to the contents of the chapter
rather than the breadth of issues covered by the company.*

Roshan

Roshan utilizes social innovation to strengthen the company and enrich society. It is creating social and economic value in a country decimated by war. Not only did Roshan create a telecommunications infrastructure from scratch, but the company has arguably been pivotal in improving the security of Afghanistan as a whole and its viability as a center for economic activity. This chapter presents Roshan's efforts to promote nation-building by developing new products and services, including mobile banking, while creating opportunities for women.

The challenge for Roshan is how to compete while adhering to its principles and dealing with on-going problems such as security and corruption. Regardless, the company has performed nothing less than an economic and social miracle in a country against all odds. It shows that, at the rebirth of a civilization, a company which creates social value is not only more likely to survive, but is likely to emerge as a dominant force.

> *"It is not like we have a choice—there is constant pressure to apply the principles of social value. Genetically these are principles of all our shareholders, especially the Aga Khan Fund for Economic Development (AKFED). These principles are, in a real (and measurable) way, rebuilding the country itself."*
>
> **Shainoor Khoja, Managing Director, Roshan Community**

In 2003 when Roshan was launched, Afghanistan was a country characterized by economic and political instability, corruption, and war. The Taliban government had collapsed in 2001 after the U.S. took control of Kabul, but insurgent pockets remained throughout the country. Education, electricity, water, healthcare, and transportation infrastructure were virtually non-existent. Mortality rates and life expectancy were among the worst in the world.

The telecom industry itself was similarly non-existent and phone calls cost $12 a minute. Within a month of the collapse of the Taliban, an offer of support for the new government came from the Aga Khan Development Network (AKDN). AKDN is a prominent non-profit operating in over 33 low-income countries, creating socio-economic growth in fragile infrastructure economies irrespective of gender, religion, or race. It provided Karim Khoja, an experienced telecom entrepreneur, as a consultant. Once in country, an opportunity arose to bid for an exclusive national telecom license. Karim applied for and won the license on behalf of AKFED, a for-profit subsidiary of AKDN that invests in private companies. Roshan, which means "light and hope," was born. As part of AKFED, Roshan is owned by AKDN and Karim Khoja has been its CEO since the beginning.

The demand for telecommunications was higher than the company had expected. The business plan had called for 150,000 subscribers within the first year; they had 70,000 within the first three months and by mid-2011 over 5 million. The country had 0.05% telecom penetration when they launched; by 2011, Roshan provided a service to over 56% of the population and competitors provided more. To meet the demand, the company needed to deal with the lack of infrastructure and security problems. Among the greatest challenges was the absence of roads and electricity, compounded by the fact that rural populations resided in mountainous regions, which made building telecommunication towers a challenge. The Taliban quickly blew up newly established towers. Roshan's construction workers had to clear landmines and build access roads before towers could be built. Electricity had to be supplied by generators, but recently the company has installed solar cells on towers, distributing the excess power to schools and hospitals.

Roshan was building infrastructure in a time of war, with violent conflict occurring regularly. To ensure the safety of its people and infrastructure in 900 sites across the country, Roshan utilized a community engagement approach. They took the radical step of asking local communities to protect the towers. Roshan paid a local "tower community" for every day the tower was not blown up. This measure resulted in a huge saving—of $13 million to date.

As it began to operate in rural regions, Roshan communicated with local elders and tribal and community leaders. Company officials explained to local leaders that Roshan could deliver important benefits including job creation, long-distance communication with relatives, and new market opportunities. Local staff were hired to help build sites and provide security. Roshan built "social sites" in areas of sparse population and high poverty, solely to improve the economies of those communities, with no expectation of financial return. Soon, Roshan was able to demonstrate that the establishment of a local phone service leads to the opening of markets, the return of agricultural trade, and the reconstruction of hospitals and schools.

In a country with a low-skilled workforce, recruitment was a challenge. However, 93% of Roshan employees are Afghan nationals with an average age of 23. The company invested heavily in employee-training in English, basic computer skills, diversity, cultural awareness, and health and safety, spending $1,500 per employee annually. This provided career mobility for staff, allowing them to move to better jobs within the company.

Roshan was value-driven from the outset. According to Shainoor Khoja, "behaviors needed to be right from the start." Today the company has a workforce comprising over 20% women. Although the challenges associated with employing women in Afghanistan would have made it easier to employ only men, the company believed that investing in women would pay dividends in the long run. The company did not offer jobs to family members of influential people or business partners. Significantly, the company did not pay bribes, or "baksheesh," a commonplace practice in Afghanistan. This carried the risk of reducing both access to opportunities and the rate of productivity, and resulted in frequent delays of supply imports by the "opportunistic" customs agency of the country.

Abductions were commonplace, but the company refused to pay ransoms. It developed a unique resolution that was remarkably successful. When an employee of Roshan was abducted, they would shut off the phone service in the region. It was well known that Roshan's policy was not to reactivate the tower until the employee was released. The local community, newly dependent on the telecom provider, soon took control of the situation and the employee was returned. According to Shainoor, "...employees who were abducted later were simply let go after their abductors saw their Roshan identity cards." Roshan can proudly say that it has never paid a single cent to the Taliban and all abducted employees have been returned.

To establish its presence across the country, the company established a flagship store in seven regions. They then essentially franchised the service to local entrepreneurs providing them with lines of credit to buy phones, SIM cards, and other supplies. They also provided training. This created 25,000 indirect jobs by 2009. The company also created Public Call Offices (PCOs) for those who could not afford phones. There were 3,900 offices by 2009, of which 95 were owned and run by women. Shainoor led an initiative to micro-finance women's PCOs where each employed one to four women. Also, a Women's Mobile Repair Center was opened with eight to nine women-owners repairing used mobile phones.

The company conducted data-driven marketing to determine the lifetime value of consumers and design product and service variations. There were no banks or ATMs in 2003 when the company launched. Roshan successfully established a service called M-Paisa, a mobile service for money transfer, payment of salaries, and micro-financing. It also launched Malomat, a system for Afghan farmers which provided transparency of commodity prices and rewards for updating prices.

Addressing the competition

Competition emerged in 2006 when Roshan's telecom license lost its exclusivity. At that time the company had a 65% market share, providing 54% of the population with coverage. However, by 2007, market share had been reduced by 44%, but Roshan was still the lead player. According to Karim, the company had become "fat and lazy." Roshan employees were using SIM cards from different companies at different times to get better deals.

Spurred by competition, Roshan added innovations such as discounts for favorite numbers, charging by the second, and new youth market features. The downward spiral in market share ceased and between 2008 and early 2009 the company gained 2% of market share.

In mid-2011 the company had five million customers and among the highest brand awareness of any company in the country. It also had a stellar record for creating social value. For example, 20% of its 1,000 employees were women—a dozen of whom were in management, the highest rate of any employer. In addition, while the company still had 70 expatriates, a third of senior management was comprised of Afghans.

According to Karim, Roshan has "lost ground, but we've regained it. People are beginning to see that this is not just a for-profit business.... This isn't just about making money, because there are simpler ways of making money."

Leadership

Today, Roshan spends $2 million annually on community initiatives. The **Roshan Community** initiative addresses critical infrastructure problems, including healthcare, water, education, nutrition, and clothing, as described below. Most initiatives have a long-term approach: for example, giving women access to computers, helping farmers to get information on markets, and providing banking to the poor. It was launched by Shainoor Khoja. Born in Tanzania and raised in England, she studied physical therapy and started successful related businesses around the world. She attained an MBA in Healthcare from City University in London and studied at Cambridge and Harvard.

Roshan's staff is very loyal to its leaders. For example, a staff member told Shainoor that the employees would literally "take a bullet" for their colleagues from abroad. Roshan and its staff are on a mission, working on project after project to rebuild the country.

Healthcare

Afghanistan faced serious challenges to healthcare, including a ratio of one medical doctor per 50,000 people. Roshan Community established a non-profit clinic that cost $1 per patient to run. By 2011, the clinic was serving 6,000 patients and provided care to Roshan employees, suppliers, and clients, as well as to expatriates from other corporations and NGOs. They launched "telemedicine," a service to allow doctors to collaborate over long distances, and partnered with a French institute to supply treatment to children with life-threatening conditions.

Water

Roshan Community drilled local wells in areas with no access to water, thereby increasing sanitation levels and the safety of retrieving water.

Education

Roshan Community set up a program to educate children working on the streets. In addition, the program taught art, tailoring, and calligraphy, and provided access to music, theater, and sports. Working with the One Laptop Per Child initiative in the U.S., the company provided 1,500 laptops for children. The children of employees were offered scholarships through to the completion of high school, with the stipulation that the children performed well at school and their parents were successful at work. This helped with staff retention as competition increased. The company spent $50,000 on the construction of playgrounds, which became social centers where vendors set up food stalls, creating economic activity.

Nutrition

The company provided 50,000 meals per month to children in five camps for returning refugees. All senior staff at Roshan worked in the soup kitchens. Children who received these meals were expected to attend school.

Clothing

The Warm Heart Initiative provided sweaters and blankets to families earning less than $1 per day. When a custom duty of 13% prevented the service from continuing, frequent international travelers were required to bring two suitcases of clothes back with them in order to continue the program, albeit at a reduced level.

Questions from students for Shainoor Khoja, Director of Corporate Affairs, Roshan

Q: Roshan's budget for community investment is only 1.6% of the budget, or $2 million. Why is the funding for community initiatives so small?

A: Our whole business model is devoted to CSR and community investment. Roshan Community's activities are in addition to the core business activities. We have engaged in many activities; as an example, we built eight flagship schools that helped us to unite ourselves with the Afghan people, to build capacity, and accelerate our expansion. One cannot look at the budget for Roshan Community as distinct from the rest of the budget.

Q: In what ways has Roshan promoted the safety of women?

A: Roshan works to ensure the safety and well-being of women in Afghanistan in several ways. First, women can call our call center for help in an emergency and the call center will mobilize the emergency services. We offer women airtime minutes "top-up" on credit should they run out while out or at a distance, that can be repaid later. All female staff are taken to work and brought back to ensure that they are safe.

We have also worked hard to promote work as an option for women, assuring the elders that women will be respected and their culture protected. All cars have GPS tracking to assure that we know where women workers are and that they are safe.

Q: Can you tell us more about Roshan's anti-bribery policy?

A: Roshan has a policy that forbids employees from taking bribes. Any item worth more than $100 which is given to an employee must be reported. Any employee who has been proven to have taken a bribe is fired. This has led to a significant cultural shift as, in the past, a procurement officer thought nothing of "borrowing" a television set that was not being used—today it is understood that this is stealing. We do not take bribes, we do not give bribes, and we do not give free phones or air time. We are trying to create a mindset shift in a culture where bribes have been business as usual.

The Taliban have said that "M-paisa [cell phone enabled banking] is a good system, as it helps people, but we don't like it because it fights corruption."

Q: What is your view on Roshan's role in the future?

A: This is a time of significant change in Afghanistan. People are getting jobs, buying apartments, cars, and televisions. However, Afghanistan has not yet reached the tipping point. This will likely take another five to ten years.

Our name means "hope and light" and was chosen by the Afghan people. Roshan is very much an aspirational brand. We are working towards prosperity for the future and we believe in the power of growth of a united Afghanistan.

Fifty-one percent of our profit is re-invested in the country, and the remaining 49% goes to shareholders. With the 51% profit we invest in the growth of Roshan, we build other projects—power plants, hospitals, and much more. We are an Afghan company that is invested in its future and we are here for the long term.

Sources

Presentation by Shainoor Khoja, Managing Director, Roshan Community, Babson, November 29, 2011.

Bhardwaj, G., D. Wylie, and M. Regele (2011) *Case Study: Roshan: A Pioneering Telecom Company in Afghanistan.*

3
Addressing environmental and social needs

In a time of economic crisis, Ford has addressed strategic opportunities in sustainability and redefined the very purpose of the company. In a move that would have been unthinkable a few years ago, Ford has partnered with a leading competitor to develop more environmentally friendly pick-up trucks. This case study examines the power of leadership, within a company and by a company, to create social value.

This chapter is based on classroom discussions and interviews from 2011 and 2012, and does not represent a totality of the activities in which the company is engaged. The diagram at the beginning of the chapter is meant to orient the reader as to the contents of the chapter rather than the breadth of issues covered by the company.

Ford

"Ford understands that, with the growing world population and the increased population density of urban areas, it is neither practical nor desirable to put every individual into a private automobile. This realization is one of the key forces driving Ford to redefine its organization as a mobility solutions company rather than an automobile company, by investing in new technologies and partnerships."

John Viera, Global Director of Sustainability and
Vehicle Environmental Matters, Ford Motor Company

Industry and company context

The U.S. automotive industry is beginning to recover from the effects of an economy in decline over the past few years. From 2006 through 2011, annual growth fell by 5.5%. As credit policies tightened, retail sales plunged. As a result and despite a government auto bailout, General Motors (GM) and Chrysler both went bankrupt. However, the industry began to show signs of recovery as revenue spiked 11.5% in 2010. The market is expected to gradually improve through 2016, but will battle the recession and high gas prices, leading buyers to likely postpone purchases of new vehicles. With steadily increasing gas prices, it is possible that consumers will continue to seek out more fuel-efficient, "green" cars for their next vehicle purchase.

Ford Motor Company is a U.S. multinational automaker, based in Dearborn, Michigan (a suburb of Detroit). The company was founded by Henry Ford and incorporated in 1903. In December 2012, Ford employed roughly 171,000 employees at 278 plants and facilities worldwide. In 2012, Ford sold approximately 5,668,000 automobiles, with net profits of $20.2 billion, making Ford the number two automaker in the U.S., number four in the world (based on annual vehicle sales), and number nine American-based company in the 2012 *Fortune* 500 listing. Ford Motor Company owns and operates two main brands, Ford and Lincoln, and owns a small stake in Mazda in Japan.

Ford's corporate social responsibility program

Ford Motor Company has been reporting on sustainability for 12 years and has a well-developed corporate social responsibility program that has earned them many accolades. They have been listed on the Dow Jones Sustainability Index's (DJSI) Annual Review of Global Automotive Sustainability Leaders. For six consecutive years to 2011, Ford was chosen for the best-in-class list. The company has been awarded six ENERGY STAR® Awards for Sustained Excellence by the U.S. Environmental Protection Agency, and Best Sustainability Reporting in 2007 by Ceres.

Ford's corporate citizenship program can be divided into three segments: environmental, mobility, and human rights. With relation to the environment, Ford has made a commitment to be best-in-class in fuel economy for every segment they participate in, while also investing in and patenting new technologies like EcoBoost fuel-saving technology. Ford seeks to decrease its environmental impact, and has reduced the energy use of its global operations by 27% (12% per vehicle built), CO_2 emissions by 31% (16% per vehicle built), and water use by more than 25% (11% per vehicle built) since 2000.

As an automotive company, mobility is a key interest for Ford. Ford responds to the challenges of sustainable mobility with several initiatives. These include developing and deploying advanced technologies, promoting road safety, and exploring new models of mobility through innovative partnerships. Furthermore, Ford understands that, with the growing world population and the increased population density of urban areas, it is neither practical nor desirable to put every individual into a private automobile. This realization is one of the key forces driving Ford to redefine its organization as a mobility solutions company rather than an automobile company, by investing in new technologies and partnerships.

On the social front, Ford is doing a lot of work with its supply base. They have translated their code of conduct into other languages to ensure that suppliers worldwide are meeting Ford standards. Ford has trained over 1,649 suppliers and assessed 709. Each of Ford's suppliers disseminates good practice to their own suppliers. In this way, Ford can create a cascading effect in the actions that they take, and can also disseminate good practice to the community at large. Ford also focuses on programs that promote workplace health and safety. The company has active personal health promotion programs in most regions where the company operates, and has deployed common global metrics across these programs.

A major product overhaul

John Viera is the Global Director of Sustainability and Vehicle Environmental Matters at Ford Motor Company, and has worked at Ford for 29 years. He has been in his current position for seven years, directing Ford's work on Global Sustainability while overseeing the advanced regulatory work, which involves negotiations with regulators relating to fuel economy. He also works with the electrification group to promote electric vehicles, building partnerships with utility companies and laying out plans to assess how many electric vehicles Ford will need to build in the next five years.

In reaction to rising gas prices in 2006, Ford leveraged all of its assets to borrow $23.6 billion. Ford recognized that if gas prices continued to rise, the demand for smaller, fuel-efficient cars would continue to rise as well. The company openly recognized that this was not a vehicle category that Ford excelled in and, to succeed, they would need a major product line overhaul. After borrowing the money, Ford accelerated down the path to transform their product line.

Ford is investing in myriad technologies, ranging from electric and hydrogen to advanced technologies like EcoBoost, that improve the fuel economy of traditional engines. Ford is faced with questions about how to reconcile its sustainability platform with the large sport utility vehicles (SUVs) and trucks that dominate its sales and are often associated with the company. Many environmental groups would prefer to see Ford abandon large vehicles completely. Considering that Ford trucks are still a major source of income for Ford, this is not a practical option. Furthermore, the American market is not ready to abandon the use of trucks. Even if Ford were to stop producing trucks, consumers would continue to purchase them and would simply give their business to a competitor. If Ford stays in the game, as John points out, and uses technologies like EcoBoost to make trucks more sustainable, the company can infuse environmental sustainability into the sector from within.

Prior to his position as the Global Director of Sustainability, John worked in operations. In that role he worked on the Lincoln Navigator, a large SUV and a bane of environmentalist groups. However, if used in a certain way, the Lincoln Navigator could be considered sustainable. For example, for large middle-class families, it doesn't make sense to own a Ford Focus because it wouldn't fit the entire family.

They would require two or three Ford Focuses, which is impractical and unaffordable. In their case, a Navigator is sustainable, practical, and more environmentally friendly than driving multiple vehicles.

John argued that there is a need to make a business case for any idea, be it environmental, social, financial, or a combination. In the case of EcoBoost on the F-150 truck, a business case was made to increase V6 power through R&D to raise V6 sales, lower emissions, and create increased business for Ford. Without the upfront analysis, this idea would not have progressed. For an idea to be adopted, one must figure out how the concept might be financed and determine the length of the return on investment. Executives want to know the final cost of the idea and the potential risks and rewards. In other words, take the pressure off the decision-maker by making an idea impossible to say no to, thereby drastically increasing the adoption rate.

Developing a new strategic vision

Another surprising revelation about Ford's sustainability program was its level of strategic planning. Many people question the sustainability of automobiles as a whole. John Viera and Ford recognize this reality, and are working to reposition Ford as a mobility solutions company, rather than a vehicle manufacturer. Every MBA program references the article, *Marketing Myopia*, in which Theodore Levitt warns about the dangers of defining a market too narrowly. He references the plight of U.S. railway companies that refused to broaden their description of their market and, therefore, lost out to the airline companies. Another example is Coca-Cola which defines its market so broadly that, even as a multi-billion-dollar company, it describes its market share as being in the single digits. John refers to Ford as a mobility solutions company and, as such, offers a strategic view that will give Ford a much better chance of adapting to and competing successfully in a rapidly changing environment.

Ford recently formed a partnership with Toyota to develop hybrid technology for full-size pick-up trucks. John describes Ford and

Toyota as **co-leading** this initiative and, in so doing, brings a new word into the lexicon. At first glance, such a partnership would seem illogical for the two companies. However, following the idea that Ford wants to differentiate on performance, John stated that he is passionate about developing solutions that will allow both companies to reduce their overall emissions. It is not about which technology drives the car, but rather how it drives and the overall driving experience. The work being done by Ford and Toyota together will have a greater positive environmental impact than if either company worked to develop such solutions alone. As more cars begin to use this technology, fewer pollutants will be released into the air, leading to a reduction in CO_2 emissions and enhanced air quality.

John has not always been concerned about sustainability; his passion evolved over time. His interest began after realizing the importance of the triple bottom line and the impact of the financial elements of a business on environmental and social issues. John was once asked to focus his attention on sustainability. He and a select few of the other executives realized that, in order to be a truly sustainable business, Ford had to further embrace the environmental and social bottom lines.

Ford is continually looking for ways to bring recycled and renewable content into the cars it manufactures. For example, it is using plant-based products in place of petroleum-based products, such as soy to make foam for seats, and denim once destined for landfill is being used to pad carpets.

Passionate leadership

Passion is a very important theme in the Babson MBA class, as it suggests that corporate social responsibility can take hold in big companies as individual leaders become engaged. One of the recurring themes expressed by many of the C-suite executives profiled in this book is that social value creation starts with the people and culture of the company. If one or two top executives become passionate about and engaged in social and environmental issues, a focus on sustainability can take root in the C-suite and become woven into the fabric of an organization. It is not necessary for the passion to already exist within the company; it can be developed and nurtured.

Questions from students for John Viera, Global Director of Sustainability and Vehicle Environmental Matters, Ford Motor Company

Q: What is Ford doing to reduce the demand for high-fuel intensity vehicles?

A: Our business model had been to dominate the market for large vehicles and trucks. We realized that, going forward, we needed to make money on small cars. Ford needed to change its product portfolio. We borrowed $23 billion from Wall Street to start producing options besides large cars. Our new CEO had come from Boeing and realized that we could not borrow enough money to create this change.

Ford needed first to make large cars more fuel-efficient, as truck owners are also interested in fuel efficiency. Our goal was to be the leader or tied with the leader in fuel efficiency in all of the markets we produce in. We needed to have breakthroughs.

To drive breakthroughs in fuel efficiency, Ford began a partnership with Toyota. Both companies would continue to compete, but the basic fuel efficiency principles would underlie both brands. Colors, interiors, and exteriors would differ but the fuel efficiency technology would be similar.

Q: You mentioned that the Navigator can be sustainable if marketed in the right way. How does Ford market the Navigator to make sure it's used in a fuel-efficient way?

A: In the past we did not produce the best small cars. So now, we have come back with good-looking small cars. Our enabler is to have better and smaller cars. In addition, we do not over-market the large vehicles to people who do not need them. Our goal is to get potential consumers into the product as soon as possible. It is important to have people who buy the product long-term. As a result, we do not want to push them into a product that is expensive to drive due to high fuel prices.

We also worked to change the mentality of the dealers. Ford produces vehicles with both six and eight cylinders. The vehicles with eight cylinders were considered the more macho of trucks. The EcoBoost technology provides the fuel efficiency of a smaller engine but with a large cylinder. It drives 22 miles per gallon but feels just like an eight cylinder vehicle.

The marketing folks were nervous as they worried that Ford would lose customers who were committed to having eight cylinders. Would these customers be willing to switch to a six-cylinder vehicle? Ford needed to change the mindset. Through its marketing efforts, Ford began to show customers that the EcoBoost series would get more power and performance with more fuel efficiency.

Q: Ford went through a major restructuring. What do you see as Ford's responsibilities to shareholders as it reduces its workforce?

A: Ford had a business that was not sustainable. In 2005, Ford had 365,000 employees, whereas it now has 165,000. Ford began by selling off brands, such as Land Rover, Volvo, Jaguar, and Aston Martin. These brands were a distraction to Ford.

The economic downturn had a major impact on our operations. In mid-2000, we sold 17 million cars per year. Nine and half or ten million represents a breakeven point. Now we sell 13 million vehicles. We can take care of shareholder needs.

Q: As you lay off workers, what kinds of benefits are in place to help workers who are terminated?

A: There were several phases. The employees who took the first severance packages got the best deals. These packages were better than the industry average. At no point did employees lose their pension plans.

Q: How do you promote higher standards in countries where standards are lower than those in the U.S.?

A: There is a very real issue for Ford around safety standards, which are often lower in developing countries than in the U.S. We do have minimum safety requirements; however, we do work to raise safety standards in countries like India. We hope one day to have global safety standards. Is a life in India or Mexico less valuable than in the U.S.?

Promoting social value creation at Ford

The students explored ways in which Ford could further enhance its social value creation work. Due to the nature of Ford's business, the company's products have a considerable impact on the environment and society, both in the manufacturing and consumption of the products. For Ford, the problem appears not to be a shortage of social value creation ideas, but rather, deciding which proposed ideas are likely to have the largest impact and are worth dedicating limited resources to.

Sources

Presentation by John Viera, Global Director of Sustainability and Vehicle Environmental Matters, Ford Motor Company, Babson, November 29, 2011.

4
Creating social value through social entrepreneurship

What kinds of leadership skills are necessary to be a social entrepreneur? How does a social entrepreneur start a company with social innovation at its core? How can **on-shoring** (relocating production in the United States) help a company differentiate itself in a crowded marketplace?

This chapter is based on classroom discussions and interviews from 2011 and 2012, and does not represent a totality of the activities in which the company is engaged. The diagram at the beginning of the chapter is meant to orient the reader as to the contents of the chapter rather than the breadth of issues covered by the company.

School House

"We made a name for ourselves because of our social mission. We have won over the hearts and minds of students and administrators who are worried about scandals."

Rachel Weeks, CEO of School House

Background

School House designs collegiate apparel which is licensed to over 100 universities and colleges in the United States and abroad, including Harvard and Duke. The company was founded with a mission to promote "fair fashion." Creating social value is embedded into the DNA of School House, driving the mission, the manufacturing process, the supply chain, and more. Social value can take many forms, and over the course of School House's life it has shifted, but has always remained at the core of the company.

Rachel Weeks was a senior at Duke University when she decided to create fashionable collegiate apparel. While a fashion-forward collegiate label was a novel idea, the real forward-thinking concept was that she would pay her overseas employees a fair living wage. Rachel founded School House in 2008 and began producing apparel in Sri Lanka. The norm of the garment industry across parts of Asia had been to pay near-poverty-level wages. Rachel worked with the factory to ensure that living wages were paid, thereby ensuring her supply chain was in line with her company's mission and commitment to "fair fashion."

In the United States, School House had made a number of successful sales at universities and bookstores. After several years in partnership with a Sri Lankan supplier, Rachel decided to "**on-shore**" manufacturing of the School House product line. Relocating the manufacturing process to the United States boosted the local economy and provided livelihoods for countless Americans struggling during a challenging economic period. With "Made in America" as a new part of its vision for social value, School House moved all primary operations to North Carolina. They now source their cotton, yarn, and fabric locally. Their shippers, packers, screen-printers, and cut-and-sew partners are all located in North Carolina. As of November 2011, School House has supported over 2,784 American apparel jobs in North Carolina across ten companies.

School House combines social value and fashion. Fashion is the force that pushes the business forward, and social value is the engine upon which it moves. While the form social value creation takes can change, School House's model demonstrates that it can remain at the heart of a business.

Challenges

Rachel Weeks has done an excellent job of starting a company with the intention of creating social value along with profits. This approach has allowed her to break into the competitive apparel market with recognizable brand marketability. If Rachel had just started a business with the intention of creating a clothing line for profit, she would have faced immense pressure from her competition. Clearly, Rachel's strategy was to put the issue of a living wage at the forefront of her business plan; this has led to the bonus of being able to market her vision and passion, and secure the financing needed to grow the company.

As the company grows, Rachel will continue to face new challenges. One of her biggest challenges will be to determine and clarify her target market. School House's "Made in America" label has a strong appeal for a broad base of potential customers and, as a result, the company chose to broaden its distribution from the typical college bookstore model to a more encompassing national retail client. Asian consumers are beginning to see the value of the "Made in America" brand, and Rachel uncovered a way to tap into this market. At the Harvard University bookstore, she observed that the predominant customers were East Asian tourists who were specifically looking for apparel that was "Made in America."

This brings up the challenge of simultaneously capitalizing on a new market and increasing the scale of her business without sacrificing the brand image. The new line will not have the level of individualization needed for a college line, which will enable them to place larger orders with their manufacturers and provide the opportunity to increase the scale of the "Made in America" apparel line in global markets. One example of this is the "Blutarsky" sweater (a reference to the iconic shirt worn by John Belushi in the movie "Animal House") which just has the word "COLLEGE" on it. This adjustment in strategy will allow School House to increase profits as it benefits from economies of scale.

When Rachel started her endeavor to bring a living wage to Sri Lankan garment workers, she was taking a risk. She was investing her own money and could easily have tried to market her innovative idea of a more fashionable line of college clothing with a standard low-paying manufacturer. By choosing to advance awareness and increase wages for Sri Lankan factory workers, Rachel was hoping to foster both social innovation and sustainable social change. As the concept of social value creation begins to evolve over the next few years, there will be more emphasis on how we categorize value.

Challenging the assumptions of social value creation

Rachel Weeks challenged many of our students' assumptions and helped to significantly shape their thinking about social value creation. Some of the assumptions they held before her in-class interview include:

Assumption #1: Social value creation is a linear process

Rachel's story demonstrates that social value creation is a journey. Building a business poses significant challenges; building one with a social mission at its core—one that makes intentional decisions to innovate in order to stay true to its values—presents even more complex challenges. Rachel frequently pivots as she navigates her way through this complex landscape. The story of School House demonstrates that entrepreneurship—especially social entrepreneurship—is not a linear process, but rather one that requires countless iteration. For example, when Rachel needed to move manufacturing from Sri Lanka to North Carolina, she had to reposition the focus of her social mission from promoting a living wage to revitalizing American manufacturing. While the issue of a living wage is still important to Rachel, and she hopes to do more in the future on that topic, business realities forced her to re-adjust.

- *Lesson learned: Social value creation is a journey*

Assumption #2: Social value creation is an add-on to your already-existing business model

Many in the class assumed that social value creation was a way to do good things in your community or the world *in addition* to your business strategy. School House demonstrates that social value creation *can be your business model*. Throughout every step of the sourcing and manufacturing process, School House makes purposeful decisions that will create value for their suppliers, manufacturers, and the local community. These actions are often more difficult and costly, but they define School House's value proposition; their "Made in America" label serves as one of the main differentiators of School House's product and gives them a competitive advantage.

- *Lesson learned: Social value creation can be at the core of your business model, and can serve as a competitive advantage and point of differentiation*

Assumption #3: You need to do well before you can do good

This is an assumption that was challenged in complex ways during the conversation with Rachel. Students wondered how a small start-up can really affect social change when it doesn't yet have the power or leverage that a large corporation does. When Rachel moved manufacturing back to North Carolina, she had difficulty influencing wages for factory workers in the United States because she did not yet have the volume or leverage to make demands of her suppliers. Rachel admitted that, while she's still passionate about the issue of a living wage, she first needs to scale up her business in order to make a real impact. This would seem to confirm the assumption that you must first do well (financially) in order to do good (socially).

However, when confronted with this challenge, Rachel did not stop trying to create social value. Rather, she shifted her focus to an initiative that was more feasible given her current resources. By focusing on the revitalization of manufacturing in North Carolina, Rachel has made a real impact on the industry and will continue to do so as her business scales up. School House's business model demonstrates that it is possible to do good while creating economic value as a small start-up, while you are still in the early stages of doing well financially.

- *Lesson learned: Doing well and doing good should be simultaneous processes if social value creation is integrated into the business model*

Assumption #4: Profit-driven business strategies aren't creating social value

Students entered the class with an assumption that profit-driven business strategies do not create social value. Similar to the prior assumption, this line of thinking led them to conclude that business strategies are either profit-driven *or* creating social value, rather than viewing them as simultaneous processes. What they realized is that perhaps the best way to create social value is through the pursuit of profit-driven strategies that leverage a company's best assets and core competencies to solve a problem.

Rachel said that, when she pitches her business to potential investors, her focus is on selling the viability of her business model and revealing the gap that exists in the marketplace for fashion-forward collegiate clothing. School House's "Made in America" label serves as a differentiator and competitive advantage for the brand, but it does not overshadow the fact that School House is filling a market need while pursuing a profit. Like all successful entrepreneurs, Rachel started by identifying a need (fashionable collegiate clothing) and delivering a solution to the consumer. What makes School House unique is the social value they create. If Rachel had attempted to innovate the textile industry in North Carolina without an independently viable business idea and a market demand, she would not have had such an impact on the industry.

- *Lesson learned: Strategies that utilize the business' core competencies to solve social problems create the most value*

Rachel Weeks as a leader

Rachel Weeks is unusual among the leaders profiled in this book in that she heads up not only the corporate social responsibility functions, but also the entire business. It is important to re-emphasize that corporate social responsibility is the core element of the School House business model. Keeping that in mind, the Boston College Center for Corporate Citizenship's Corporate Leadership Competency model (which is mainly focused on an individual working within a large organization) provides a good framework to examine and analyze Rachel's leadership traits and how they relate to School House today and to its future (Pinney *et al.* 2009).

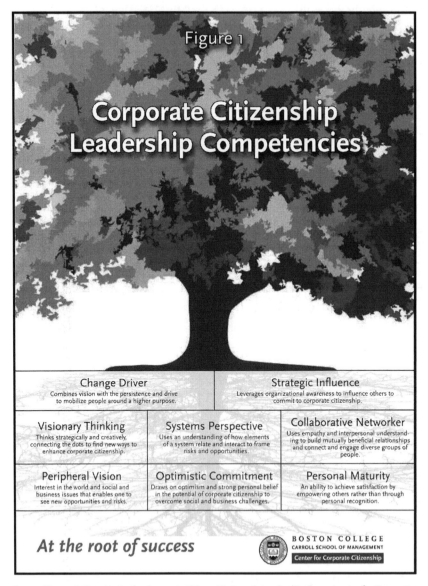

Source: Boston College Center for Corporate Citizenship (2010), *Leadership Competencies for Corporate Citizenship: Getting to the roots of success* (Boston College Center for Corporate Citizenship, www.BCCorporateCitizenship.org).

Personal maturity

An ability to achieve satisfaction by empowering others rather than through personal recognition. (Self-reflection and learning from the past constitutes personal maturity.)

Rachel Weeks has a high level of personal maturity. During her presentation, she spent a significant amount of time discussing the lessons she has learned from many of the decisions she has made since starting School House. This self-reflection has enabled Rachel to make more informed decisions. Rachel also achieves satisfaction by empowering others rather than through personal recognition. For example, she understood that the factory owners in Sri Lanka should receive credit for providing a living wage.

Peripheral vision

Interest in the world and social and business issues that enable one to see new opportunities and risks.

Rachel's decision to **on-shore** demonstrated that she has a high level of peripheral vision. When things began to go poorly in Sri Lanka, she saw the opportunity to move production to the United States. Now, Rachel and her team are located in close proximity to most of the factories and are able to maintain higher quality standards than they could at a distance.

Optimistic commitment

Draws on an optimistic and strong personal belief in the potential of corporate citizenship to overcome social and business challenges.

Rachel considers all manufacturing challenges to be surmountable. Her passion and optimistic commitment have helped her to overcome challenges that could have undermined the growth of the company.

Collaborative networker

Uses empathy and interpersonal understanding to build mutually beneficial relationships, and to connect and engage diverse groups of people.

Rachel provided several examples of how she uses networking to build mutually beneficial relationships while connecting and engaging with diverse groups of people. First, she utilized collaborative networking to find a mentor in Sri Lanka who provided her with invaluable help navigating and setting up School House's production. In the United States, she worked with several female Chief Executive Officers to help her overcome some of the challenges she faces as a female executive. Rachel utilized collaborative networking to secure funding for the company; by networking with a diverse group of angel investors, she made sure she was aware of their objectives, ranging from advancing corporate social responsibility to simply making a profit.

Systems perspective

Uses an understanding of how elements in a system interact, to frame risks and opportunities.

The apparel eco-system is continuously shifting. In the past year, the world has watched in horror as factories in Bangladesh and Pakistan have either collapsed or burned, taking the lives of thousands. The unprecedented nature of these disasters show the degree to which Rachel was able to successfully assess risk and relocate production to the United States from Asia. She might have relocated production to either Pakistan or Bangladesh, but was able to use a systems perspective to develop an innovative solution: **on-shoring**. She understood the context in which she wanted to operate.

Establishing a living wage for domestic workers requires a systems perspective. To develop a framework in which a living wage could be paid, Rachel needed to develop a systems perspective that encompassed a wide range of partners.

Conclusion

The means of creating social value differ between existing corporations and start-ups. Existing corporations have certain resources available in order to initiate their efforts, while School House and other start-ups tend to have access to limited resources: most notably, financial resources. While Rachel founded School House with the intention of keeping the living wage mission at the core of its business model, she soon needed to re-adjust her mission in order to grow her company. She focused on a different way to create social value by bringing manufacturing back to North Carolina. She realized that her first priority for School House was to establish a strong revenue model. Following that, she would have the capacity to be more ambitious with her social value creation efforts, perhaps returning to her commitment to promoting a living wage.

Large corporations often have the marketing resources to advertise or communicate their social value message or efforts to their consumers. However, many small start-ups, including School House, cannot engage in conversation with their consumers due to financial constraints, thereby leaving to interpret much of the company's brand and values by themselves. Small companies like these risk alienating or confusing customers who may not realize or appreciate their approach to social value creation.

Corporate citizenship is much harder to integrate into an existing corporation than into a start-up. Rachel continues to embed corporate citizenship into the four domains of the business: products and services, operations, community engagement, and governance. While "Made in America" is Rachel's ultimate strategy, she also delivers quality apparel through more ethical manufacturing operations and through a greener, home-grown supply chain. She has skillfully moved her operations to the U.S. and has engaged her community successfully by supporting close to 3,000 jobs. While it is true that Rachel was unable to continue to pursue her vision for a living wage in Sri Lanka due to financial constraints and various challenges, she successfully re-created her business strategy with the same corporate citizenship framework in a way that creates real social value in her home state of North Carolina.

Sources

Presentation by and Panel Interview with Rachel Weeks, at Babson College, November 20, 2012, https://babson.webex.com/babson/lsr.php?AT=pb& SP=TC&rID=14202727&rKey=41832be6d76ee440&act=pb

SchoolHouseInc YouTube Channel, www.youtube.com/watch?v=iWTWCu2 EURg&feature=plcp

Pinney, C., S. Kinnicut, Hay Group and S. Spencer (2010) "Leadership Competencies for Corporate Citizenship: Getting to the Roots of Success," Boston College Center for Corporate Citizenship, www.gosw.org/files/planning_results/Leadership%20Competencies%20for%20Community%20Involvement%20-%20Getting%20to%20the%20Roots%20of%20Success.PDF, August 2013.

Pinney, C., S. Kinnicutt, S. Spencer, and A. Callahan (2009) *Leadership Competencies for Corporate Citizenship: Getting to the Roots of Success* (Boston College Center for Corporate Citizenship and Hay Group, www.bcccc.net/index.cfm?fuseaction=document.showDocumentByID&DocumentID=1352).

Leipziger, D. (2012) *Case Study: The Aspen Institute* (School House), www.shopschoolhouse.com

5
Social innovation in hiring and PathMaking

Greyston Bakery's mission is to combat poverty in the surrounding community of Southwest Yonkers, New York. As a social enterprise, Greyston Bakery uses its policies to hire people who are difficult to employ and trains them for opportunities at the Bakery and in the community. This chapter examines how a company can foster an environment which supports employees by providing access to affordable housing, daycare, and healthcare. Greyston Bakery is New York State's first Benefit Corporation and has been a pioneer in creating social value for over three decades.

This chapter is based on classroom discussions and interviews from 2011 and 2012, and does not represent a totality of the activities in which the company is engaged. The diagram at the beginning of the chapter is meant to orient the reader as to the contents of the chapter rather than the breadth of issues covered by the company.

Greyston Bakery

"We don't hire people to bake brownies; we bake brownies to hire people."

Greyston Bakery's mission[1]

Background

Few social enterprises have been around as long as Greyston Bakery; which has a rich 30-year history as a successful and innovative social enterprise. Founded in 1982 by Bernie Glassman, Greyston Bakery specializes in gourmet brownies and has a vision to end poverty in

1 www.greystonbakery.com/wp-content/uploads/pdf/greyston-bakery-guiding-principles.pdf

Southwest Yonkers, New York, by combatting homelessness and chronic unemployment. Thirty years later, poverty still exists in Yonkers, but in addressing the root causes of poverty and providing pathways to a better future, Greyston Bakery's mission has been revolutionary.

After struggling to earn a significant profit during the early years, a lucrative contract to supply the brownie bits for Ben & Jerry's ice cream allowed the company to grow into a $10 million business. Employees are compensated fairly and receive health benefits along with career development training. Greyston Bakery has an **open-hiring** policy and focuses on providing work for those who have limited job experience. Employees are trained to develop transferrable skills that can be used to secure their next position.

Although Greyston Bakery is a for-profit entity, it promotes workforce development and is part of an integrated network of organizations based in Yonkers which provide community development support to the area. The Greyston Foundation supports initiatives related to affordable housing, health and family services, and child and youth services. Successes over the years include:

- Development of over 300 units of permanent housing for homeless and low-income families in Westchester, New York

- Formation of a nationally accredited pre-school childcare system to support low-income families

- The creation of a permanent housing and daycare program for local families affected by HIV/AIDS

- Community gardens which address the food desert (or lack of access to healthy foods)

In February 2012 Greyston Bakery became the first **benefit corporation** to register in the state of New York. This followed a successful $7 million debt restructuring process, which resulted in a boost in revenue and the means to hire an additional 30 employees.

The Greyston Foundation plans to continue its expansion in order to increase its impact in the community. In addition to scaling out their employment and childcare centers, plans exist for additional real estate development projects and the launch of a new social enterprise as a means of diversifying the organization's revenue mix. Another recent development is the inclusion of solar energy in the Greyston Bakery baking process. The rooftop 36-panel solar array was donated by Green Mountain Energy's Sun Club, an organization that promotes solar power and assists socially responsible organizations with the reduction of their carbon footprint.

Open-hiring

Greyston Bakery's **open-hiring** policy is an excellent example of social innovation. They employ many people who have never had a job before, including recent immigrants, the disabled, people who have been incarcerated, or those leaving drug rehabilitation programs. Greyston Bakery keeps a list of people looking for a job and contacts them when an opening becomes available. By law, they are required to check if the candidate is a U.S. citizen, but no other background checks are made. Through **open-hiring**, the company has transformed the lives of people in the community and built a pool of motivated workers.

Managers train apprentices with an emphasis on punctuality and respect for authority. Approximately 60% of the apprentices do not stay with the company. Those who do, go on to earn highly prized jobs with benefits, a rarity in Southwest Yonkers.

Delaney Philogene is a good example of the success of **open-hiring** at Greyston Bakery. She fled her native Haiti as a teenager, lived on her own from the age of 14, and left school after becoming pregnant. She was determined to find employment and went to Greyston Bakery daily to put her name on a list for a job opening. After starting on the assembly line, she secured a full-time position in accounting and later moved into an accounting position at another company.

Creating systemic change

The success of the open-hiring policy used by Greyston Bakery is based on the company's efforts to create systemic and enduring change. The policy provides jobs to people in need as part of a holistic approach which includes improved access to affordable housing, healthcare, and childcare.

Greyston's founder, Bernie Glassman, is a former NASA aerospace engineer who became a Buddhist monk and has infused a Buddhist perspective into the company. Bernie's view that everything is highly inter-connected and central to the company's strategy and success. Bernie began with a deep knowledge of the community he was trying to serve. He and members of the Greyston team volunteered at a local soup kitchen, trying to understand the world of the homeless. By volunteering, Bernie made an important discovery: many of the homeless people in Yonkers are single parents. Without access to childcare, these homeless parents could not find work and were unable to break out of a life of poverty. Without a job, they could not attain housing. It was a vicious cycle that lasted many generations, and the despair surrounding this cycle often led to drug addiction, which required further access to help. It would be very difficult to foster job creation without addressing the broader issue of a lack of quality childcare, housing, and training. Those suffering from HIV/AIDS were in need of additional services. The inter-connectedness of these problems led Bernie to develop the Greyston Mandala, which creates a network of services provided by the Greyston Foundation that holistically and systematically address poverty in the community.

Bernie created the Greyston Family Inn, funded by wealthy patrons in Westchester County, which gave members of the community access to permanent housing for the first time. Then Greyston received a grant from the New York State Housing Assistance Program to buy and refurbish a deserted building just a few blocks from the bakery. In most cases, construction would have taken place with an outside contractor. But with so many people willing to work, Bernie hired local people to refurbish the complex. By being involved in the construction of the edifice, local people took pride in their work and were trained in valuable skills.

PathMaking

One of the core concepts Bernie infused into the company was the concept of **PathMaking**. Inherent in this concept is that all people are on a progressive path in their lives. Greyston Bakery trains people to work hard, makes them "employable," and then facilitates their advancement to other fields. Each employee has a life plan and works towards its fulfillment. The company helps employees achieve their goals, whether that involves working towards a GED (General Educational Development) diploma or getting advice on healthcare. Greyston Bakery is a stepping stone, and employees are encouraged to go on to higher-paying jobs, such as working to repair air-conditioning units.

In 2013, Greyston opened a **PathMaking** Center inside the bakery. The Center has a full-time director who assists employees and everyone within the Greyston Mandala with tools to work towards self-sufficiency. The Center provides access to computers and technology training, tutoring, counseling services, career advancement, GED, and college prep classes.

Greyston Bakery provides an excellent example of **sector blur**: the blurring between the roles of government, civil society, and business. Where addressing poverty and homelessness was once the purview only of governments, business can work to **co-create** solutions to urban poverty, HIV/AIDS, and food deserts. Bernie Glassman is an example of a **boundary-spanner**, working across boundaries to develop new models for addressing social problems through business.

The relationship with Ben & Jerry's

In the first few years of its existence, the bakery grew and faced challenges. A defining moment came in 1987 when Bernie Glassman was introduced to Ben Cohen of Ben & Jerry's. The ice cream maker decided to purchase brownies from Greyston Bakery to make ice cream sandwiches. Ben Cohen recalls receiving the first shipment of brownies which were all stuck together in giant 50-pound rocks. The ice cream company tried to create ice cream sandwiches and ended up with tiny brownie pieces. What could be done with tiny brownie pieces? From this fiasco, came a new flavor: chocolate fudge brownie made with pieces of Greyston Bakery brownies.

One of the central ideas behind Ben & Jerry's is **linked prosperity**, a notion that, as a company grows, it should share its resources with its employees, its business partners, and the local community. Ben & Jerry's is a values-led business, taking a stand on a wide range of issues from helping dairy farmers and promoting Fair-Trade to climate justice and peace building. Ben & Jerry's long-term partnership with Greyston Bakery has thrived, in part, because both companies are values-led companies working towards **linked prosperity**.

In 2001, the British–Dutch conglomerate, Unilever, bought Ben & Jerry's. To this day, the company remains a wholly owned subsidiary of Unilever and, in 2012, became a Certified B Corp. Greyston Bakery reports that the company is inspired by "the prolific efforts of Unilever and its Sustainable Living Plan."[2]

The Greyston Bakery value chain

Greyston Bakery is part of a value chain that includes its suppliers and its main customer. Greyston Bakery's 2012 Annual Benefit Report names Unilever's Sustainable Living Plan and Ben & Jerry's **linked prosperity** vision as two key influences on the company's vision for creating social value. When Unilever acquired Ben & Jerry's, the ice cream company became a wholly owned subsidiary with its own

2 Greyston Bakery, B Corp report, 2012, p. 17.

board of directors. Over the course of many years, Greyston Bakery and Ben & Jerry's have developed "layers of alignment,"[3] aligning values and mission. Unilever's unique ten-year Sustainable Living Plan provides Greyston Bakery with a useful framework:

Enhancing livelihood

Goal: to source 100% of agricultural raw materials sustainably.

This area focuses on sustainable sourcing and improving the lives of farmers and distributors in Unilever's supply network. Between 2010 and 2011, sustainably sourced raw materials increased by between 14% and 24%; and the company has the goal of engaging with 500,000 small-scale farmers and 75,000 small-scale distributors by 2020.

Reducing environmental impact

Goal: to halve the environmental footprint of products.

The focus is on the reduction of greenhouse gases, improvements in water quality and efficiency, and a lower waste footprint. Although, to date, Unilever's environmental impact has largely remained the same, their programming goals are mostly on target.

In 2005, Ben & Jerry's became the first of its kind to use Fair-Trade certified ingredients. Unilever aims to source only Fair-Trade ingredients for the ice cream by 2013.

Benefit corporations and B Corps

Greyston Bakery is one of the most well-known social enterprises and it is both a Certified B Corp and a benefit corporation. B Corps are certified by the non-profit B Lab to meet rigorous standards of social and environmental performance, accountability, and transparency.[4] A **benefit corporation** is a legal entity designated by each state and

---

3 The authors are grateful to Miguel Padro from The Aspen Institute for coining this useful term.

4 www.bcorporation.net/what-are-b-corps

is required to generate social value. "**Benefit corporations** are not a trend, but it is the direction in which business is moving," says Ariel Hauptman of Greyston Bakery.

Definitions:

Benefit Corporations[5] "are a new class of corporation that 1) creates a material positive impact on society and the environment; 2) expands fiduciary duty to require consideration of non-financial interests when making decisions; and 3) reports on its overall social and environmental performance using recognized third party standards."

B Corps[6] "are certified by the nonprofit B Lab to meet rigorous standards of social and environmental performance, accountability, and transparency. Today, there is a growing community of more than 850 Certified B Corps from 28 countries and 60 industries working together toward 1 unifying goal: to redefine success in business."

In February 2012, Greyston Bakery became the first benefit corporation to register in the state of New York. A year later they filed their first B Corp report.[7] In 2008, Greyston Bakery chose B Lab to evaluate its impact and see how it compares to other social enterprises. See page 77 for comparative data.

Conclusion

Greyston Bakery provides an excellent base from which to understand social innovation and social enterprise. As a **benefit corporation**, it

---

5 benefitcorp.net
6 www.bcorporation.net/what-are-b-corps
7 www.bcorporation.net/community/greyston-bakery-inc/impact-report/
   2011-02-03-000000

has taken on the challenge of continuous innovation, not only within the company, but within its value chain and beyond. Greyston Bakery aims to expand the social innovation of **open-hiring** to other companies in a wide range of sectors. To quote Ariel Hauptman, Greyston Bakery's Business Development Manager, the company is asking an unusual question for a bakery: "What can we teach American Express?"

Greyston Bakery's guiding principles

"We don't hire people to bake brownies; we bake brownies to hire people."

Greyston Bakery operates with a double bottom line. We prioritize both profits and our social contributions. We strive to be a sustainable model for inner-city business development. Our **open-hiring** policy and apprenticeship program provide both jobs and training for individuals who have struggled to find employment in the past. When we generate profits, we use them to fund the community development programs of Greyston Foundation. In order to operate effectively, the bakery's leadership commits itself to the following explicit principles. These principles all flow from Greyston's overall mission.[8]

- The bakery will strive to be a model for inner-city business development committed to Southwest Yonkers. The bakery will remain at the forefront of the field of inner-city business development, continuing its unique success, and actively disseminating information about the model. It will do this in Southwest Yonkers, the inner-city community where it was created and has grown, and where there is a high concentration of

8 www.greystonbakery.com/wp-content/uploads/pdf/greyston-bakery-guiding-principles.pdf

hard-to-employ individuals. Any expansion elsewhere will only be undertaken if the Yonkers base of operation remains strong.

- The bakery should consistently achieve an operating profit. Achieving operating profit is the best route to long-term survival of the organization, and the best inducement for others to follow the bakery's model. Furthermore, because they are subject to the discipline of market competition, bakery employees, unlike participants in many well-intentioned job-training programs, develop skills that are genuinely valuable.

- The bakery will maintain an **open-hiring** policy. The bakery will continue its **open-hiring** policy, and the associated apprenticeship program, in order to provide opportunity to Yonkers' hard-to-employ population. Providing jobs, and training for those jobs, to individuals who would otherwise likely be unemployed is one of the greatest benefits that the bakery provides to the community.

- The bakery will actively integrate itself into the Greyston Mandala. Bakery management will work with the Greyston Foundation to give factory employees opportunities to take advantage of the **PathMaker**, childcare, housing, and other services. In addition, the bakery will attempt to provide professional opportunities for individuals who enter Greyston through other parts of the Mandala.

- A central purpose of the Greyston Bakery is to generate profits that can help sustain the work of the Greyston Mandala. The Bakery's net profits will support the various non-profit projects of the Foundation, the bakery's sole shareholder. The amount will be balanced against the need to reinvest in the business to remain competitive and the need to maintain a certain level of available working capital at all times.

- The bakery will rigorously measure, document, and monitor its progress toward all non-financial goals. The bakery will monitor the success of its **open-hiring** policy, skill building efforts, employee turnover, and other social goals.

- The bakery will empower its employees by compensating them fairly for their efforts and move towards a living wage. The bakery will pay employees fair wages for their skills. While for some employees this salary may not currently constitute a "living wage," the bakery is committed to working with these individuals to improve their skill set and value. To this end, the bakery will provide training opportunities so that employees may increase their earning power. In addition, the bakery will promote from within thereby providing opportunities for higher earnings. The bakery will also encourage and support employees who seek outside vocational training, academic advancement, and professional non-bakery-related enrichment. Finally, the bakery will also support employees who seek greater self-sufficiency through employment elsewhere.

- The bakery will strive for stable employee turnover rates for post-apprenticeship employees. The bakery will not attempt to achieve artificially high employee turnover in order to free up staff positions for new employees, as maintaining a profit under this constraint is not possible. However, because of the bakery's **open-hiring** policy, the turnover rate of the newest employees may exceed the norm.

- The bakery will automate its production whenever such changes are fiscally appropriate. In order to maintain a profit and to assure that bakery employees are developing skills valuable in the modern marketplace, the bakery will automate its production when fiscally appropriate. The bakery management will monitor applicable technological trends in the baking industry in order to inform automation decisions. The bakery will strive to maintain and increase employment levels, despite increased automation, through improved marketing efforts and sales growth.

- The bakery will support the individual growth of its employees through its **PathMaking** program. **PathMaking** is built on a holistic concept, provides individuals within the Greyston community with personalized support to a more successful life as defined by the individual. With the support of a counselor and life skills training in areas such as money management, nutrition, and parenting, each person will develop their own Path to self-sufficiency.

Greyston Bakery, Inc. 2013 B Impact Report

Certified **(B)** Corporation	Company Score	Average Score*
Overall B Score	135	80
Environment	19	9
Environmental Products & Services (e.g. Renewable energy, recycling)	0	4
Environmental Practices	18	6
Land, Office, Plant	5	4
Energy, Water, Materials	9	2
Emissions, Water, Waste	4	1
Suppliers & Transportation	<1	N/A
Workers	18	22
Compensation, Benefits & Training	13	15
Worker Ownership	0	2
Work Environment	4	4
Community	83	32
Community Products & Services	0	15
Community Practices	81	15
Suppliers & Distributors	4	4
Local	3	5
Diversity	N/A	2

Certified **(B)** Corporation	Company Score	Average Score*
Job Creation	36	2
Civic Engagement & Giving	N/A	4
Governance	15	10
Accountability	12	6
Transparency	4	3
Overall	135	80
80 out of 200 is eligible for certification		

* Of all businesses that have completed the *B Impact Assessment*

Sources

Greyston Bakery (2012) "Bakers on a Mission: Benefit Corporation Report," www.bcorporation.net/community/greyston-bakery-inc/impact-report/2011-02-03-000000.

Glassman, B., and R. Fields (1996) *Instructions to the Cook: A Zen Master's Lessons in Living a Life that Matters* (New York: Bell Tower).

Interview between Deborah Leipziger and Mike Brady, CEO Greyston Bakery, February 12, 2013.

Interview between Deborah Leipziger and Ariel Hauptman, Business Development Manager, Greyston Bakery, April 5, 2013.

6
Co-creating new sources of recycled materials

Social value creation is a journey, a pathway, and this chapter examines how a social entrepreneur has designed a new range of products through Entrepreneurial Thought and Action®. Eric Hudson is an example of an entrepreneurial leader. Preserve® provides an example of co-creation of new sources of recycled materials.

This chapter is based on classroom discussions and interviews from 2011 and 2012, and does not represent a totality of the activities in which the company is engaged. The diagram at the beginning of the chapter is meant to orient the reader as to the contents of the chapter rather than the breadth of issues covered by the company.

Preserve

> *"Preserve is 'proof of concept' for a new way of doing business.*
> *Preserve is a model for other companies due to its pioneering work*
> *in creating sustainable consumer products and bringing together*
> *like-minded companies to create recycling systems for their products."*
>
> **Jay Coen Gilbert, Founder of B-Labs**[1]

Background

At its core, sustainability is about design. Preserve® is a story of how companies can incorporate sustainability in every element of the business, from what they produce to how they produce it. In 1996, when

---

1 Preserve Media Kit, www.preserveproducts.com/media/presskits/Pre serve_MediaKit_2012.pdf

Preserve was founded, "green products" were being made out of wood. There were a handful of products made out of recycled plastic, and most consisted of ashtrays and penholders. The majority of companies did not consider their carbon footprint, yet Preserve had the foresight to create new systems and partnerships that enabled the design of sustainable products.

Preserve collects plastic from individuals and companies, and re-engineers it for its products. Conventional plastics, made from oil and natural gas, contribute to roughly 9% of the world's petroleum usage.[2] In contrast, Preserve's products are developed with recycled #5 polypropylene plastics, which require significantly less water, coal, oil, gas, and electricity for their production.

The Preserve Toothbrush, the company's first product, features a handle made entirely of 100% recycled plastic. Preserve has since expanded its line into kitchen, personal care, and tableware products, with toothbrushes and food storage containers topping the list of best-sellers. Preserve items can be found in over 7,000 merchant locations, including such mass retailers as Target and Whole Foods.

Preserve integrates sustainability into its strategy and brand value. The company found a way to connect and engage with its consumers, also known as **preservers**. They are encouraged to return their used toothbrushes to be converted into plastic lumber for tables, benches, and boardwalks. Preserve aims to develop a long-term relationship with **preservers** by selling toothbrush subscriptions: packs of toothbrushes to last an entire year. This new way of marketing engages people over time and builds brand loyalty.

In addition to using recycled materials, Preserve demonstrates a commitment to the environment throughout every facet of its operations. Harmful toxins are kept out of products and animal testing is strictly forbidden. Offices are powered by wind and lit by sunlight in order to reduce energy consumption, while U.S.-based manufacturing operations means no CO_2 emissions are generated by international

2 www.preserveproducts.com/aboutus/index.html

transport. Finally, Preserve supports local environmental and community organizations with marketing efforts and staff commitments.

The following comprise the company's core principles:

- Preserve products are made from 100% recycled plastics and 100% post-consumer paper. By using recycled materials, the company saves energy, preserves natural resources, and creates an incentive for communities to recycle

- All plastic products are recyclable, either through postage-paid labels and mailers (toothbrushes and razor handles) or at the curb in communities that recycle #5 plastic

- Products are made in the United States to reduce shipping distances and fuel consumption, limiting the environmental footprint

- No animal testing

- Preserve products are made to last—and to look good doing it[3]

Entrepreneurial Thought and Action® (ET&A)

Babson College uses the methodology of Entrepreneurial Thought and Action® (ET&A) as a framework to teach students how to think and act as entrepreneurs. Essentially, the framework breaks down the process of entrepreneurial thinking into two mindsets: prediction and **Creaction**.

Prediction is "a pattern of thinking and acting based on the assumption that the future is going to behave in a way similar to the present and the immediate past."[4] Predictive reasoning is an instinct that develops at a very young age, and people continue to use it every day of their lives. In business, prediction might determine which stocks to include in a portfolio, the best candidate to hire for an open position,

---

3   www.preserveproducts.com/aboutus/index.html
4   Schlesinger, L., C. Kiefer, and P. Brown (2012) *Just Start: Take Action, Embrace Uncertainty and Create the Future* (Boston: Harvard Business School Publishing): xviii.

or which supplier to select for a new contract. When developing a plan for a new business, particularly if the product or service is entering a new market, the level of uncertainty can be quite high. It can be tempting to spend a lot of time in the early planning stages, carefully researching the industry and trying to account for every unknown element, in order to avoid being caught off guard. This is where a lot of would-be business owners get stuck.

Serial entrepreneurs spend time thoughtfully making predictions, but they also employ **Creaction** to quickly move on to the next important stage of starting a business.

Creaction is a combination of the words creation and action, and refers to the process of taking a small step towards a goal, then evaluating the response before making the next decision. Instead of spending valuable time and resources gearing up to make a big investment, entrepreneurs can make small, meaningful movements towards their goals and easily change course along the way, if necessary. **Creaction** leaves room for predictive error. By taking small actions, the entrepreneur can be nimble and make adjustments to a product or strategy if something fails to go as planned. The process looks like this:

- Act
- Learn (from that action)
- Build (on that lesson), and act again[5]

ET&A is the process of using prediction and **Creaction** together. Preserve provides an excellent example of how entrepreneurs like Eric Hudson employ this type of thinking when building a company.

ET&A and Preserve

After graduating from Babson College, Eric worked as a management consultant, specializing in maximizing operational efficiency. At the same time, he began exploring ways to combine his interest in

5 *Ibid.*

industrial design with a desire to be environmentally resourceful. Eric researched different types of plastic, their potential to be recycled, and local sourcing options. After settling on a business model, he turned his attention towards developing his first product: a new toothbrush design.

During the mid–1990s, Reach® was the dominant player in the toothbrush market. The distinctive, forward-angled head may have set it apart aesthetically from other brands, but Eric questioned whether it was effective at brushing throughout the entire mouth. He began speaking to dentists and other professionals in oral hygiene, and learned that 95% of them recommended a different model. He began conducting his own research and found that, when the curve of the toothbrush was reversed, brushing became much more effective. Not only did this design have the potential to revolutionize the industry, but as the entire population brushes their teeth daily, there was an opportunity for a toothbrush made of recycled materials to appeal to the 45% of the population who recycle. Furthermore, toothbrushes must be replaced every so often, providing the opportunity to benefit from brand loyalty and a steady demand.

Figure 5.1 **Preserve Toothbrush model vs Reach® brand**

Source: www.drugstore.com, www.coupongeek.net[6]

Eric used predictive thinking during the early days of Preserve. He conducted research on current technology and sourcing, considered the types of product that would fit best with his business strategy, and

---

6   Preserve Toothbrush: www.drugstore.com/products/prod.asp?pid=94977& catid=183804&aid=338666&aparam=goobase_filler&device=c&network= g&matchtype= Reach toothbrush: www.coupongeek.net/2011/03/reach-toothbrush-or-floss-coupon.html

dreamed up a new design for a common item. He did so while continuing to work as a consultant, exploring one area at a time, and gradually discovering how all of the pieces fit together. Although Eric had a solid grasp of the type of company he wanted to create, he knew to seek out experts in order to fine-tune his ideas. Eric **Creacted** by reaching out to area dentists and sketching out an initial blueprint. After finalizing his own design, Eric again brought his idea to dental professionals to refine the concept. Each small step he made led to another.

Utilizing the right materials was key to the success of his fledgling company. Eric needed a type of plastic that was affordable and safe both for the environment and consumers. Luckily, the University of Massachusetts Lowell, one of the country's leading innovators in plastics technology, was located nearby. Eric was able to meet with specialists, manufacturers, and moulders, and determined that polypropylene (or #5) was the plastic that best suited his needs. In addition to being a safe, food-grade material, it is also recyclable, allowing Eric to engineer his product using exclusively re-processed plastic.

At first, it appeared as though the Preserve Toothbrush was preparing to enter the market at the perfect time as nearly 50% of Americans recycled. While other companies were introducing green products, they were not producing them with recycled materials, leaving the marketplace essentially empty. However, any sense of reassurance was quickly dashed in June 1996 by the publication of John Tierney's "Recycling is Garbage," in the Sunday edition of the *New York Times*. The 7,000-word tome harshly criticized recycling programs as unnecessary, ineffective, and financially burdensome, and broke the newspaper's hate-mail record.

Mandatory recycling programs aren't good for posterity. They offer mainly short-term benefits to a few groups—politicians, public relations consultants, environmental organizations, waste-handling corporations—while diverting money from genuine social and environmental problems. Recycling may be the most

wasteful activity in modern America: a waste of time and money,
a waste of human and natural resources.[7]

The article created quite a stir at the time, and caused Eric to question whether his business plan had potential. Would other anti-recycling articles be published, creating a new trend in journalism?

Eventually the buzz surrounding Tierney's article died down, and Eric pushed forward with his fledgling business. Initial purchase orders were low (first-year sales amounted to just $70,000), but Eric considered that to be a success. As the company continued to grow, it became necessary to hire a team.

ET&A and establishing a team

Initially, Preserve operated as a company focused on environmental rather than social change. During the first ten years of operations, employees joined because they believed in the mission. As a small start-up with a small staff, there was always much to do and too little time, lending itself to a project-based environment. Collaboration was encouraged, and employees learned new skills through trial and error. The same principles of predictive thinking and **Creacting** that helped Eric launch his business, continued to apply as his workforce began to grow. By wearing multiple hats, staff members developed into innovative thinkers, and Eric is quick to point out that, even when projects failed, the team still benefited by learning something new.

As the scope and scale of Preserve's business continued to expand, it became necessary to hire specialists rather than generalists. Although a team-based approach to problem-solving was helpful during the early days when everyone was still learning on their feet, it eventually became inefficient for staff to set their work aside to focus on one problem as a team. Transitioning into a streamlined division of labor approach to operations simply made more sense. Today, Preserve is

7   Tierney, J. (1996) "Recycling is Garbage," *New York Times*, June 30, 1996.

comprised of 11 employees. The company website proudly proclaims that they "bike, walk, train, and drive (some in hybrid cars) to our office outside of Boston intent on bringing Preserve and our mission into more homes every day."

Becoming a B Corp

Preserve became certified as a B Corp in October 2011, and has been recognized by B-Lab as one of the "Best of the Best for the Environment." Eric credits his employees with leading the effort to become certified as a B Corp. The team immersed themselves in accurately measuring and accounting for all of their operations, and relished the opportunity to have Preserve recognized for what makes it so unique. When areas of low performance were discovered, efforts at improvements were made. Eric describes it as a process that was very enlightening, and resulted in bringing new company policies to light. Overall, Preserve scored highest in areas of accountability, environmental practices, and sourcing.

Eric's relationship with his board of directors is also key to the company's success. Although it remains primarily focused on maintaining a positive financial cash flow, the directors also understand Preserve's influence as part of a movement to create social change. Eric also acknowledges the effect his board has had on his evolution as a CEO. Often, the social mission of the organization will pull him in many directions, and his board of directors has stepped in to encourage him to regain focus. In order to remain effective, Preserve needs to make the best of its resources. As a for-profit business, there is a limit to the amount of exploration that can take place.

ET&A and partnerships

Gradually, Preserve began to make a name for itself as one of the major **influencers** in the recycled products movement. As its popularity increased, Eric began to receive feedback from customers who pointed out a frustrating problem. Although they loved being able to purchase items made from re-used polypropylene, consumers often could not recycle their own discarded #5 containers because many community programs would not accept them. The material is one of the most common forms of packaging (found in most yogurt, hummus, cottage cheese, and other containers), but municipalities struggled to sell salvaged items because the re-sell market was so small. As a result, many #5 plastics ended up in landfills, contributing to the very problem that Eric had set out to solve.

Luckily, Preserve was in a good position to help. Not only was the company invested in reducing landfill waste, but they now also had an opportunity to dramatically improve their supply chain. By directly collecting #5 plastics, the very material they needed to produce their product, the company could provide a recycling solution for its consumers, directly contribute to improving the recycling rates of #5 materials, receive direct access to their inputs, and increase their profile within the community. Preserve partnered with Stonyfield Farm, a business best known for their organic dairy products (and a major consumer of #5 plastics), to create the Gimme 5 program. Participating retail locations would be drop-off locations for #5 plastics and would send them to Preserve to be used in their production. Those who wished to participate, but did not have access to a drop-off location, were invited to mail their containers directly to Preserve. As a final incentive, Gimme 5 partnered with a company called Recyclebank, which offers rewards to participants of green initiatives.

Preserve could not have tackled this problem alone, and Eric describes the company as having a "penchant for partnerships." By working alongside Stonyfield Farm, Brita, Recyclebank, and participating retail drop-off locations, they were able to co-create a new partnership and establish what is recognized as a ground-breaking program in extended producer responsibility. This team-based approach is sure to continue in the future. Preserve is expanding globally, with products currently sold in 18 countries. Success will be based on their ability to continue sourcing and manufacturing locally.

Developing partnerships in new regions will allow the business to remain profitable and impactful within each community it enters.

Mutual influence

Eric uses the term "mutual influence" when he talks about the evolution of Preserve as a company. The plastics experts at University of Massachusetts Lowell influenced Eric and vice versa. By using recycled materials in products, Preserve influenced what was possible. There was mutual influence between Stonyfield and Preserve, as well as with the design firms that helped to build Preserve products. In a kind of ripple effect, the design firms used by Preserve received new business and were able to generate new products for other companies. According to Eric, "we can make a bigger difference with more partners and friends." Like Greyston Bakery, Preserve aims to create a network of socially minded companies.

Conclusion

When asked what advice he has for current MBA students who are wrestling with whether to follow a similar path, Eric responded positively. He encourages entrepreneurs to follow their passions when building their businesses. Eric was passionate about finding solutions to the increasing levels of landfill litter in the country (or re-using the materials that more and more consumers were recycling), and was able to translate that into a profitable business. Preserve creates value in many ways: for society, the environment, for its owners, and for preservers. As Preserve continues to grow, its sphere of influence widens. Although his initial goal might have been to reduce waste, Eric did not just create a recycling company, he created a revolution.

Sources

Interview with Eric Hudson by Cheryl Kiser and Deborah Leipziger, March 27, 2013.

Schlesinger, L., C. Kiefer, and P. Brown (2012) *Just Start: Take Action, Embrace Uncertainty and Create the Future* (Boston: Harvard Business School Publishing).

Tierney, J. (1996) "Recycling is Garbage," *New York Times*, June 30, 1996, www.nytimes.com/1996/06/30/magazine/recycling-is-garbage.html?pagewanted=all&src=pm.

www.preserveproducts.com/aboutus/index.html

www.voiceamerica.com/guest/8295/eric-hudson

7
Sustainability by design

How can companies not only use design to create social value, but also use their communications strategies and leadership position to address social problems? This chapter explores how Target acts as an influencer, impacting public policy issues like drug addiction and safety in the community, while redesigning the retail experience.

This chapter is based on classroom discussions and interviews from 2011 and 2012, and does not represent a totality of the activities in which the company is engaged. The diagram at the beginning of the chapter is meant to orient the reader as to the contents of the chapter rather than the breadth of issues covered by the company.

Target

"We need to build sustainability into the design of everything we do, from products and services to addressing the needs of the community."

Nate Garvis, Author of *Naked Civics*,
Advisor to Target

Background

George Dayton founded the Dayton Dry Goods Company in 1902, on the principles of: dependable merchandise, fair business practices, and the generous spirit of giving. The first Target store opened in 1962 and Dayton Dry Goods was finally renamed Target Corporation in August 2000. Currently there are 1,850 stores worldwide,

1,784 Target stores in 49 U.S. states and 66 stores in Canada. Target has branded itself as an up-scale, discount, one-stop shopping destination to purchase general merchandise, apparel, home goods, food, and more.

The company was founded with an unwavering commitment to keeping social value at the forefront of the company's priorities. Since its inception, Target's core mission has focused on engaging with and creating social value for local communities. Since 1946, Target has given 5% of its profits to the communities where it does business. Today, it has reached a significant milestone of donating more than $4 million per week to its local communities. Target's belief is that, by helping to build strong communities, the customers and team members who live in those communities will in turn help build a strong business.

In 2012, *Fortune* magazine ranked Target #25 on its list of the "World's Most Admired Companies" and #1 for General Merchandisers.[1]

Creating social value for 50 years

Target's social value creation focuses on four main areas:

Sustainability

Target aims to create stores that are sustainable by design and run responsibly. The company will have sixteen LEED (Leadership in Energy and Environmental Design) certified stores in the United States by fiscal year-end (FYE) 2013, and is pursuing certification for all 124 stores opening in Canada in 2013. The company strives to use resources responsibly and to maintain the health of its neighborhoods. Target has increased the number of sustainable products it

---

1 www.money.cnn.com/magazines/fortune/most-admired/2012/snapshots/
   2303.html

offers in its stores, and promotes re-usable bags and recycling among its customers and team members. The company has set several environmental goals, including improving packaging for its own Target Brand products and reducing its carbon footprint by 15% by FYE 2015.

Great place to work

Target makes its employees (or "team members") a top priority. The company invests in career development with training and mentoring programs, talent management, and regular performance reviews. An internal initiative offers programs and incentives to provide team members with the tools and resources to be healthy individuals. Target also encourages employee volunteerism, exceeding 679,000 volunteer hours at FYE 2012. The company creates internal volunteer competitions to boost internal levels of volunteerism. Target also works to promote diversity and inclusion in its stores and at corporate headquarters.

Safety and preparedness

Target strives to make its stores and neighborhoods safe and secure for its team members, communities, and guests (as Target refers to its customers). The company has a robust network of relationships with first responders throughout the world, and provides resources and tips to promote awareness about how to react in an emergency. The company wants to ensure that employees are prepared for both local and global emergencies.

Education

The company's educational programs aim to help children read proficiently by the end of third grade, which is a critical milestone on the path to high school graduation. They accomplish this through a variety of channels, including grants, book donations, library renovations, and donations from employees and customers.

Target acknowledges that there are still areas that need improvement. In its 2011 Corporate Responsibility Report, the company explicitly stated its goals for FYE 2015 to include:

- Increasing the sustainable seafood selection to 100%

- Increasing the number of ENERGY STAR certified stores to 75%

- Improving transportation efficiencies by 15%

- Increasing the number of staff diabetes screenings to 91%

- Increasing support of education programs to $1 billion

The existence of these goals exemplifies Target's commitment to incorporating social value in its mission, products, operations, and the community.

Target as an influencer

Social value creation is about addressing social dilemmas. Target's deep roots in the community help the company to be an **influencer**. The controversy around the sale of some over-the-counter drugs provides a concrete example of how Target can influence public opinion and public policy to address social and community problems. In the late 1990s, serious social and environmental problems associated with the sale of over-the-counter drugs containing pseudoephedrine (PSE) emerged. Medicines sold to fight coughs, colds, and allergies were being bought, and in some cases stolen, by drug dealers and addicts to make methamphetamine, an illegal substance, also known as "meth."

Retailers such as Target faced a serious problem—they were unknowingly complicit in the scourge of drug addiction. Not only was drug addiction a serious threat to the communities in which Target is located, but the manufacturing laboratories have high levels of chemical contamination. Target and other retailers were faced with twin social and environmental problems.

Nate Garvis, who worked on public policy issues at Target at the time, understood that it would be years before medicines could be reformulated to avoid the use of PSEs. Nate saw the need for action and said plainly to the President of Target, "If we do not act, it will hurt Target." Nate advocated that Target should work with law enforcement and activists to develop a solution. According to Nate, "You're either at the table or you're on the menu." Target decided it was better to work in tandem with other interested parties and co-create a solution.

In 2005, Target became the first retailer to voluntarily place medicines containing PSEs behind the counter. In a press release, Target announced its decision and informed the public that it would require a Target salesperson to provide these medicines.

Nate recalls this turning point: "This was not a popular day for me. We were about to upset Moms and burden our stores. The medicines bring in approximately $350 million in revenues and here I was, trying to limit customer access to the medicine. Don't expect that creating social value will make you popular right away. People like to be tethered to the familiar."[2]

Communications is a vital part of social value creation. The communications strategy around PSEs needed to be thoughtful and deeply ingrained, not just an afterthought. As Nate says, "communications are like cheese—it cannot just be sprinkled on top but needs to be built in to the process, like lasagna." Target developed a plan to communicate to stores and then to its customers. The next round of communication was to work with policy-makers to integrate Target's experience into decision-making at the national level. By being at the table, Target was able to play a role in defining U.S. legislation, which was built around Target's best practice.

2 Interview between Nate Garvis and Deborah Leipziger, January 18, 2013.

Target's close relationship with the communities in which it is based helped the company to communicate with concerned stakeholders. Nate recalls Target's approach to customers: "We told Moms that we did not want to inconvenience them, but we don't want your kids to grow up in neighborhoods where meth is a serious problem, leading to high drop-out rates and increased crime." By communicating directly to concerned customers, Target began to see that parents were pleased that the company was taking into account the need to foster a safe community and to be socially relevant. While convenience is important, parents particularly recognized that a safe community is even more important. The communication strategy allowed for an alignment of values between parents, the community, and Target.

The manner in which Target dealt with the challenge of PSE had significant design implications for systems, IT, workflow, and communications. Design is more than product design, and it needs to be integrated into every aspect of operations in order to create a culture of social value creation.

According to Nate, "everything works off of a relationship." There is the relationship with the back-of-the-store team that makes everything operational, the relationship with the sales clerks whose jobs become more complex, and the relationship with customers who are somewhat inconvenienced. Nate's role in Target at that time was to be a "**curator**"—to curate the relationships with the various constituencies. "You don't make yourself relevant, others make you relevant." Another major lesson was that the good deeds initiated by Target created the opportunity for more relevance.

Target's approach to PSE provides an excellent example of **co-creation**. Target worked with public policy officials to **co-create** policy and legislation, and the approach to PSEs was devised in relation to an on-going relationship with the Commissioner for Public Safety. Salespeople were in charge of **co-creating** and developing the policy. "No one should have the hubris to think that they can pull this off alone. In many instances, action starts from a place of unpopularity. Part of the art of influence is that people cannot be forced to be involved, they need to be enrolled."[3] Change agents such as Nate Garvis at Target need to create influence strategies. It all starts from a position of "you need to trust me." Target's message is that the company can be trusted because it has a history of listening and acting.

Target was one of the first responders in the PSE crisis. The result was that sales increased and the company received a great deal of media coverage which further promoted the Target brand. The FBI gave Target a Community Leadership Award for a range of reasons, including its efforts to ensure that medicines containing PSE were sold in ways that do not endanger the community.

Leadership is a two-way street

To integrate Target's commitment to social value creation throughout its culture, the company's managers need to be competent in building strong teams that understand and execute Target's mission. Shawn Gensch, the Senior Vice President of Marketing, articulated that "social value creation is part of the company's DNA."[4]

With the vast array of information published today, Target understands that employees want to hear, not read, the company's commitment to social value creation and be able to engage in social value creation efforts directly. Target realizes that the biggest influence on customers' decision-making and perception are the people with whom they most frequently interact. Therefore, to maintain Target's authentic voice, it is essential that all team members understand Target's impact on the local community, experience the impact, and are able to communicate the company's role in the community.

---

3 Source: Nate Garvis, in class discussion
4 Interview with Shawn Gensch, Babson College, November 27, 2012.

Leadership is an integral part of Target's efforts to create social value. The best leaders do not take themselves too seriously, and are approachable to the members they lead and the customers they serve. Leadership is a two-way street. By being approachable, leaders build stronger teams and receive significantly more honest feedback. In turn, that feedback can be utilized to create changes that enable the company to better understand and serve its internal and external stakeholders. From a new employee's first day of work to the highest level of senior leaders, Target is determined to spread its mission throughout the organization's culture.

Team members give Target its authentic voice

Target is in a unique position of being able to touch thousands of lives every day, and Shawn estimates this impact reaches millions of people during the busy holiday season. Shawn stressed that simple advertisements and marketing campaigns do not do enough to maintain Target's reputation as a company that cares about the local community. Rather than marketing campaigns, the company relies on its internal team members to convey its social value creation efforts through conversations with customers. The retail industry generally has a high employee turnover, making it a challenge to maintain an authentic voice as an overall brand, particularly regarding social value initiatives.

To bring this authentic voice to the store floors, Target maintains its socially focused culture throughout the company's hierarchy, making it clear at every level that its commitment to social value and sustainability by design is unwavering. Nate Garvis describes the process of Target's work to create social value as acculturation: the act of turning an activity from a vertical to a horizontal, from specialty to ubiquitous.

To ensure that every Target employee is dedicated to social service and community, the company celebrates those who create value.

Shawn stressed that there is a difference between appreciating and celebrating. Appreciating is just hype. Celebrating, however, fosters an individual's commitment to Target's values. Long after leaving the company, team members feel that what they did matters to society, creating a sense of loyalty to the company as consumers and fellow community members.

Social media

Shawn distinguishes between marketing and social media in a compelling way. In traditional forms of marketing and branding, the company tells you a story. In social media, the communication is one-to-one. Social media is a powerful branding tool for Target, as its customers are brand enthusiasts. One of the recent hires within Target is working on **shared media**.

> **Shared Media** *is the documented engagement between a brand and a user where that engagement is reflected in both of their networks and not fully owned by either entity. In layman's terms, when you like or comment on a brand's status update or post on the wall of a brand's Facebook page, a physical record of your action now exists on both the brand's page and your personal profile. The brand doesn't exclusively own the content, nor do you. The content is partially owned and partially earned. Since that gets a little confusing, it's better to think of that content as now being* **Shared Media.**[5]

The following info-graphic demonstrates the different types of media, and shows how **shared media** exists at the center:

5 www.allfacebook.com/shared-media-facebook_b17296

Figure 7.1 **Different types of media**

Source: www.allfacebook.com/shared-media-facebook_b17296

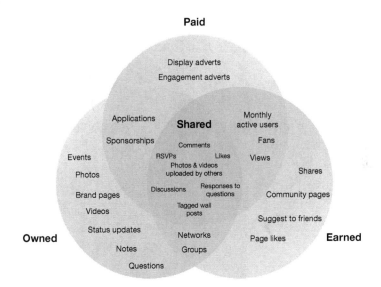

Shared media allows for a conversation—which allows companies to build consumers into the design process. This "design response" allows Target to differentiate itself.

Storytelling, both internally and externally, plays a key role in promoting the brand and making the company relevant. Leaders working to create social value need to be good storytellers, so they can inspire action and commitment from their team. Shawn is a brilliant storyteller, sharing his passion and enthusiasm in authentic ways within Target, and within the wider community. The brilliance of Target's messaging is that it creates multipliers—the teams in stores, the customers, and the local groups which receive assistance from Target, all become storytellers and brand enthusiasts.

Targeting the future

With its strong focus on local communities, Target works to address locally relevant issues. For example, one community might care a lot about environmental issues, while another might care more about literacy. Target will invest in each community in a targeted way to address their specific needs.

Another way Target can influence social value creation is through its supply chain. The company has done this in a number of ways already, but an ambitious sustainability effort could result in cost savings, and easily translate into shared value.

Within the organization, Target might consider empowering its employees to take an active role in the non-profit community, volunteering, serving on boards, and contributing creatively to charitable organizations about which they are passionate.

Finally, Target should create a series of metrics to measure its progress in the future. It is increasingly important for a large organization like Target to understand how effectively it is creating social value.

Questions from students for Shawn Gensch, Senior Vice President of Marketing at Target

Q: Describe the corporate culture at Target. What does social value creation mean for the company? How is it translated down to team members?

A: Target's commitment to social value creation is unwavering and is part of the DNA of the company. Social value creation is part of our brand promise, alongside "great design" and "expect more, pay less." We need to realize that the most impactful person to a new team member coming into Target is the person they are around most often. It isn't their direct leader and it isn't their most senior leader within their local environment. A store team leader manages 190 to 250 team members depending on seasonal ebbs and flows in staffing. That store team leader has a great impact in their community. They are the ones who are very active in the community, but maybe an hourly team member wouldn't see that person as the most impactful to them. Who they would find to be impactful is who they are spending time with, which may be a team leader, it could be a lead cashier, or it could simply be a friend. It's about making sure that everyone understands the local impact of Target's giving.

From a giving perspective and a service perspective, it's all happening in the local communities. We didn't just sell the story that Target appreciates your service or appreciates your caring for the community; we actually celebrate it. There's a difference between appreciating and celebrating. It's ultimately going to be that individual commitment to it that we hope lives well beyond any association with Target. It's when they leave us that they carry that with them. I think you have to be a celebratory culture in order for people to have a personal connection. Otherwise I think it's just hype.

Q: Could you describe Target's relationship with its supply chain?

A: When I talk about sustainability, I focus a lot on the operations side. When we talk about "sustainability by design," we are talking about responsible sourcing and what are we doing to make sure the supply chain is not causing any negative impacts. Certainly, if you think of the retail landscape, Target has an amazing portfolio of its owned brands, but many of the items available at Target are manufactured by other companies. It is necessary to make sure that there is responsible sourcing throughout the supply chain. We have the most direct impact on our own apparel, brands, or packaging. There's a very robust learning process underway with our product design team and our global sourcing teams to make sure we are responsible in finding the right providers and making sure the practices of those providers are ethical.

Q: In 2009, Target launched the "Bulls Eye Gives" initiative where it let Facebook fans vote on which charities receive Target's 5% Net Income donation. That seems like a good way of connecting Target's

social value initiatives with its community. Can you comment on whether or not that was a successful campaign?

A: It was very successful. At the time we did it, Target was at about 2 million fans and it was a 10%, or 200,000 voter getter. Today we are over 20 million, so the growth of social media has really expanded who we are and who the occasional voters are versus the advocates of the brand are. So it was wildly successful and we still continue to use it around our educational commitment. An important question, however, is: how do brands or retailers create a personal relationship through social media? It will always be important to build a personal relationship. This is different from how marketing works—with marketing you say what you are and everybody interprets it. Now, in a social space, a company says I want to be one with you. People want a response and to know that they are being heard. So, that's a new place for big brands to be, and there are still some social challenges when you don't control the message.

Q: What are some of the challenges that a large enterprise, like Target, faces when engaging in community and stakeholders around social value creation?

A: One of the challenges we face is being perceived as authentic in our response. So much of what we've done, we do at the local level. We literally will put the decisions around giving into the local community and the leaders within that community. Most companies do not localize these decisions; instead they maybe do it at the allocation level or the headquarters level. We invest in the communities in which we are operating. We believe the communities have to be healthy for our team members to be successful and healthy and for our guests and the demographic of that community to remain healthy. I think it's a challenge for companies to find an authentic voice with which to engage in the conversation and not having it be viewed as marketing.

Sources

www.money.cnn.com/magazines/fortune/most-admired/2012/snapshots/2303
   .html
Interview between Nate Garvis and Deborah Leipziger, January 18, 2013.
Interview with Shawn Gensch, Babson College, November 27, 2012.
www.allfacebook.com/shared-media-facebook_b17296

8

Creating shared success

As technology evolves and its markets mature, Verizon is undergoing a period of massive change, attempting to identify where its future growth opportunities lie. The company has developed the concept of **Shared Success** to leverage the power of its networks, technology, and people to create long-term shareholder value by addressing the needs of the communities it serves. By employing its core competencies to develop products and services that address social needs in education, energy efficiency, and healthcare, Verizon seeks new markets and revenue opportunities.

This chapter is based on classroom discussions and interviews from 2011 and 2012, and does not represent a totality of the activities in which the company is engaged. The diagram at the beginning of the chapter is meant to orient the reader as to the contents of the chapter rather than the breadth of issues covered by the company.

Verizon

"We believe that using our talent and technology to address society's biggest challenges will both grow our business and change the world for the better."

Lowell McAdam, Chairman and Chief
Executive Officer, Verizon

Introduction

In the United States, Verizon is a major player in wired telecommunication, cellular communication, video, and internet service. As the Social Value Creation Manifesto developed by the authors states (see page 5), companies need to incorporate social value creation into the design of their products, operations, and strategic vision. Verizon creates social value by developing products and solutions that address social needs such as healthcare, energy efficiency, and education. The company is an example of how social value creation can be transformative for both the company and the communities it serves.

This chapter explores Verizon's journey towards social value creation. Since 2011, when the Babson MBA class began to analyze social value creation among leading companies, Verizon has undergone significant transformation. This chapter describes the process by which Verizon has created a focus on innovation to drive social value creation, and how the Verizon Foundation promotes innovation.

Verizon's strategy, known as **Shared Success**, works to:

> *Identify and accelerate the deployment of technology solutions that create the greatest shared value, resulting in increased revenue and quantifiable social impact; and use innovative philanthropy to accelerate the deployment of our technology into underserved communities to become an incubator of social change.*[1]

Verizon is able to "leverage its networks, technology, and people"[2] to create social value in the long term, by focusing on the needs of customers and communities.

Identifying new markets

Verizon continuously seeks to identify the new markets that will sustain its business by gaining an understanding of the problems facing society and uncovering how technology can address these challenges. In particular, Verizon seeks to create business and social value by:

- Improving energy efficiency

- Improving access to healthcare

- Enhancing educational opportunities

---

1 Verizon website: www.responsibility.verizon.com/shared-success/2012
2 responsibility.verizon.com/assets/docs/2012-verizon-corporate-responsibility-supplement.pdf

The Babson–Verizon partnership

The Lewis Institute and Babson Social Innovation Lab are pleased to be part of Verizon's process of fostering innovation. The Babson–Verizon partnership began in 2011 and has been an integral part of the company's journey toward social value creation. The partnership has helped to guide Verizon's Shared Success program. Shared Success has been integrated into many high-level activities within Babson, including the management program for all first-year undergraduate Babson students as they design their own businesses, a video for the MBA classes, and the global high school program run by Babson. Verizon executives have participated in Babson's Energy and Environment Conference, and Babson is working to help the company measure its impact on society.

To understand how Verizon developed its Shared Success framework, it is helpful to begin with Verizon's work to promote accessibility.

Corporate citizenship through the lens of shared value

It is estimated that almost 11 million people in the United States are hard of hearing or functionally deaf.[3] Over half of these people are over 65 years old.[4] United Nations projections estimated that, in 2005, 16.7% of the U.S. population would be over 60 years old, and that percentage is expected to grow to 26.4% by 2050.[5] This presents an opportunity and Verizon has been building its strategy to respond.

For years, Verizon has been working to address the connectivity challenges of people with disabilities. The Verizon Center for Customers with Disabilities (VCCD) allows customers to communicate with Customer Care Representatives who are fluent in American Sign

3 www.jdsde.oxfordjournals.org/content/11/1/112.full
4 *Ibid.*
5 www.realising-potential.org/stakeholder-factbox/
   disabled-people-worldwide

Language using videophones. A customer from Maryland claims this method makes him certain that he is being understood.[6]

The company has launched a variety of innovations in recent years, including mobile devices to serve seniors who struggle with hearing loss and a technology that converts text into speech on cell phones for those who are blind or visually impaired. In addition, they have partnered with the National Braille Press to develop a wireless book reader. Verizon is continually looking for ways to increase their competitiveness in the accessibility market.

Clearly, these are not just nice things to do. Verizon aspires to build the company's competitive advantage by creating long-term value for shareowners. Yet they are also solving challenges for a growing segment of our population. Enabling the population to be connected brings value to society.

Verizon's work to promote accessibility was a precursor to its **Shared Success** strategy. According to Kathy Brown, former Senior Vice President of Public Policy Development and Corporate Responsibility at Verizon, "our work with the disability community clearly demonstrated that products and services customized for consumers with special needs created both social benefits and business opportunity. So many of the features sought by this customer segment were found attractive to the even larger senior sector; for instance, larger font size on screens, louder voice volume, and simpler navigation. This work helped lay the groundwork for our broader **Shared Success** strategy. We are now focused on creating similar value in the education, energy efficiency, and healthcare markets."

What is shared value?

Globally respected business strategy professor, Michael Porter, has led the conversation on business strategy and shareholder value creation for many years. He is now committed to reshaping the business landscape and redefining what value creation means. Together

6   www.responsibility.verizon.com/home/stories/accessibility

with author and consultant Mark Kramer, Porter has developed the idea of *shared value*. They define shared value as "corporate policies and practices that enhance the competitiveness of the company while simultaneously advancing social and economic conditions in the communities in which it sells and operates."[7] Porter believes that "incorporating societal issues into strategy and operations is the next major transformation in management thinking."[8]

Consistent with the work of Porter and Kramer, Verizon has developed the idea of "Shared Success." This chapter will explore Verizon through the lens of shared value and highlight examples of shared value in action.

Figure 8.1 **The concept of shared value**

Source: Professor Michael E. Porter, Babson CSV presentation

The Concept of Shared Value

> **Shared Value**: Corporate policies and practices that enhance competitiveness of the company while simultaneously advancing social and economic conditions in the communities in which it sells and operates

- Create economic value by creating societal value
  - What is good for the community is good for business
- All profit is not equal. Profit involving shared value enables society to advance and companies to grow faster

- Concern with societal issues will be a defining characteristic of the post-crisis era
- Incorporating societal issues into strategy and operations is the next major transformation in management thinking
- Shared value thinking represents the next evolution of capitalism

7 Presentation by Michael Porter, "The Role of Business in Society: Creating Shared Value," Babson College, Wellesley, November 13, 2011.

8 *Ibid.*

Conventional versus corporate social value

According to Porter, many companies have adopted a narrow model of building economic value in response to the "conventional needs of conventional customers."[9] Downsizing, outsourcing, and relocating are seen as strategies to increase profit, while revenue is driven through acquisitions. Societal issues do not factor into the corporate framework.

Through its **Shared Success** program, Verizon seeks to identify and accelerate the deployment of technology solutions that create the greatest shared value (increased revenue and quantifiable social impact). In addition, Verizon is using strategic philanthropy to support its entry into new markets.

Creating social value through solutions

In 2012, Verizon focused its efforts on developing solutions that promote energy efficiency and healthcare quality. Both are measured in terms of business value and social value. Business value is measured through the traditional means of revenue generation and market penetration, while social value is more difficult to accurately assess. Verizon plans to track its social value through developing measures for increased awareness and efficiency of energy solutions as well as increased access, reduced costs, and improved care in the healthcare sector.

Through its philanthropic work, Verizon is catalyzing innovation to address social needs. The company's corporate responsibility work serves as an accelerator, and its technological expertise provides innovative solutions and contributions to segments of society that provide direct social value. As stated on their corporate website: "We are reinventing our networks around mobility, broadband, and global connectivity to create a platform for long-term growth not just for us, but for America and the world." Verizon's mission

9 Presentation by Michael Porter, "The Role of Business in Society: Creating Shared Value," Babson College, Wellesley, November 13, 2011.

and strategic business model both focus on several areas of **Shared Success**.

Energy efficiency

The U.S. economy is only 14% energy-efficient. This means 86% of the energy used is lost through the production cycle and not recycled back into the ecosystem. Additionally, worldwide, information and communication technology (ICT) produces approximately 2% of the total greenhouse gas (GHG) emissions.[10] The GeSI SMARTer2020 report estimates that ICT could facilitate a 17% reduction in global carbon emissions by 2020 through smart energy, building, and transport systems. Verizon has piloted several projects that leverage its technological expertise to address these issues, including:

Networkfleet project   Verizon partnered with device manufacturers to create a wireless sensor which was connected to vehicles in the Eastern Municipal Water District's (EMWD) fleet, allowing the client to track its energy usage and, ultimately, minimize energy consumption across the fleet. GPS routing was introduced to reduce the idling time of vehicles, optimize transportation routes, and provide more efficient dispatching of service vehicles. The Verizon technology also provided continual remote emission monitoring, allowing the EMWD to track the performance of the vehicles within the fleet with a real-time data set.

This project produced very positive results over a six-month period. The EMWD realized savings as a result, optimizing both labor and fuel

---

10 The Boston Consulting Group (BCG) on behalf of the Global e-Sustainability Initiative (2012) *GeSI SMARTer 2020: The Role of ICT in Driving a Sustainable Future* (gesi.org/assets/js/lib/tinymce/jscripts/tiny_mce/plugins/ajaxfilemanager/uploaded/SMARTer%202020%20-%20The%20Role%20of%20ICT%20in%20Driving%20a%20Sustainable%20Future%20-%20December%202012.pdf).

consumption, and generated $80,000 in fuel savings and $340,000 in saved labor costs. Furthermore, it provided a significant reduction in CO_2 emissions providing a cleaner environment for the community. Verizon was able to generate revenue through the adoption of its technology while creating social value through improved energy management and emissions reduction for the EMWD.

Energy management

The ENVISION Charlotte project, North Carolina   Verizon partnered with Duke Energy to use long-term evolution (LTE) technology to introduce more transparency into a community's energy system which, in turn, allows consumers to make well-informed decisions about personal energy consumption. They created a visual platform that displays energy consumption within commercial buildings in Charlotte's urban core. Building tenants can clearly and simply understand how their actions affect energy consumption, thereby facilitating smarter decisions on energy use.

The goal is to reduce overall energy usage by 5%. Initial results of the ENVISION Charlotte project have been so impressive in helping to drive energy consumption down that the project is considering expanding into other areas such as water usage. This pilot embraces the vision and strategic mission of the company while demonstrating that Verizon's technology can create social value through improvements in energy efficiency for the community.

The next generation of healthcare

The healthcare ecosystem is continually evolving as new regulations and increasing costs of care impact the current framework. The burdens on physicians, patients, and private/public insurance providers can be eased by restructuring the current care service model to incorporate more innovative technology. Verizon has the vision to utilize their information and communication technology capabilities to both provide social value and generate a new revenue stream for the corporation within this segment of the economy.

mHealth   With mHealth, Verizon seeks to leverage its telecommunication expertise by partnering with device manufacturers to produce devices that have wireless biometric monitoring capabilities. The technology helps patients to manage chronic diseases, such as diabetes, by allowing patients to record their vitals in a wireless device that sends the results directly to their physician, providing continual, real-time data. This capability to actively manage chronic diseases could revolutionize the healthcare industry.

- *Disease progression and quality of care can be more closely monitored and thus vastly improve and reduce costs for both the insurance companies and the patient.*

- *The quality of life (QOL) of the patient can be enhanced as a result of continual monitoring that enables the physician to deliver proactive care. Proactive care can reduce complications and additional healthcare burdens.*[11]

WellPoint   This trial with Verizon employees provides a virtual video platform, allowing an employee to consult with a physician from a remote location and eliminating the need to physically visit a local primary care physician or specialist. This could be attractive to patients in rural communities who are far away from their physician, to mobility impaired patients, and to people unable to take time away from their job to seek out care.

- *The accessibility of care could improve patient compliance of treatment and improve their quality of life.*[12]

The technologies and advancements in mHealth and WellPoint can provide tremendous social value while generating revenue for Verizon. However, unlike the concrete metrics available in the energy

---

11 Source: Chris Lloyd of Verizon.
12 Ibid.

management sector, QOL metrics for demonstrating the social value of healthcare technology are much more challenging to measure. The complexity of delivering data on savings to the healthcare ecosystem presents another challenge. These hurdles need to be addressed as Verizon and the healthcare sector continue to transform the way in which the medical community innovates their service model.

Reimagining philanthropy to be an incubator of social innovation

Verizon has fundamentally changed the role of its philanthropic strategy. The new strategy seeks to understand the ways in which the company can work with its non-profit partners to learn how social challenges create market opportunities and, ultimately, how the company can create business and social value through its **Shared Success** initiative. Under the leadership of Rose Stuckey Kirk, Verizon's Vice President for Global Corporate Citizenship and President of the Verizon Foundation, the Foundation has implemented a new model focused on supporting Verizon's entry into new markets in education, energy efficiency, and healthcare. "The Verizon Foundation aims to become an incubator for new social solutions to demonstrate the efficacy of Verizon's products in real-world settings while accelerating deployment of our technology to underserved communities."[13] The new approach is to provide technology to leading non-profit partners and measure the efficacy of Verizon's products in addressing challenges faced by underserved communities.

The Verizon Innovative Learning School (VILS) program is one example of how the Foundation is supporting the business' goal to enter new markets in meaningful ways. The goal of VILS is to transform teaching and learning by helping teachers use mobile technologies in the classroom that boost students' interest and achievement in

---

13 Verizon website: www.responsibility.verizon.com/shared-success/2012.

science, technology, engineering, and math (STEM). Through VILS, Verizon is partnering with administrators and teachers in 24 under-served schools across the United States. The program provides schools with a comprehensive, year-long sequence of on-site and online professional development courses in leveraging mobile technology for teaching and learning. The International Society for Technology Education (ISTE), a Verizon grantee, trains educators to facilitate, model, integrate, and apply existing mobile technologies that support digital-age STEM learning. The VILS program also equips one educator at each school to serve as a technology coach and role model to his or her colleagues as they challenge themselves to grow professionally.

The results have been impressive: 59% of teachers were individualizing instruction more than before the program, and 37% of the students were able to increase their level of academic achievement in science and math.

The Foundation is creating similar initiatives with its non-profit partners in healthcare and energy efficiency. By implementing this novel in-kind model, the Foundation is developing valuable knowledge for how Verizon can develop new products and services that address community challenges.

Opportunities from a corporate social value framework

Porter suggests that there are three levels of shared value: re-conceiving customer needs, products, and markets; redefining productivity in the value chain; and supporting local cluster development.

By focusing on applying their technology to new markets, Verizon is working to create greater social value today and in the future through improving healthcare data availability and connectivity. Significant emphasis has been placed on creating Electronic Medical Records (EMRs) for all Americans, and pressure has come from new healthcare legislation to digitize all medical records. While this lofty goal is needed, there are many challenges in implementing these networks.

Verizon aims to add social value by making the data created by these EMRs more accessible to doctors around the country.

"The Verizon Health Information Exchange is a new service that will consolidate clinical patient data from healthcare providers and translate it into a standardized format that can be securely accessed over the Web, regardless of the IT systems the providers use."[14]

Imagine a world where you walk into an emergency room in California and the doctors are able (with your permission) to access your clinical records from your primary care physician in Massachusetts. This would enable all of us to live healthier, longer lives by receiving improved medical treatment, and Verizon would gain a foothold in a growing and vital industry.

Why does it matter?

As Porter and others have pointed out, the corporate culture in the United States has become focused on short-term returns at the expense of long-term sustainable value creation. Companies frequently defer investments to bolster quarterly returns while communities, individuals, and the environment suffer. Many have come to see business as the problem.

Yet the authors see the corporate community as uniquely positioned to create its own economic success while addressing important societal dilemmas. By stepping in where non-profits and government entities lack the capacity to act, business can build meaningful solutions through new philanthropic models, business operations, and strategy.

The case of Verizon demonstrates that this approach:

1. Opens new opportunities for economic value creation through the use of technology (e.g., increasing the connectivity of the hearing and vision impaired; developing telemedicine and technologies for promoting energy efficiency)

14 www22.verizon.com/about/community/va/technology/tech_index.html

2. Enables companies to experiment with different philanthropic models and non-profit partners to incubate new solutions

3. Solves pressing challenges facing society (e.g., decreasing healthcare costs)

4. Pushes Verizon to create an innovative business model that can respond to an ever-changing market climate

Perhaps more than at any other time in history, we need the power, creativity, and resources of the corporate sector to address crucial societal dilemmas. The framework of Shared Success is one way to accomplish this.

Sources

Presentation by Christopher Lloyd, Corporate Responsibility, Verizon, November 20, 2012.
Verizon website: www.responsibility.verizon.com/shared-success/2012
responsibility.verizon.com/assets/docs/2012-verizon-corporate-responsibility-supplement.pdf
www.jdsde.oxfordjournals.org/content/11/1/112.full
www.realising-potential.org/stakeholder-factbox/disabled-people-worldwide
www.responsibility.verizon.com/home/stories/accessibility
Professor Michael E. Porter, Babson CSV presentation
Presentation by Michael Porter, "The Role of Business in Society: Creating Shared Value," Babson College, Wellesley, November 13, 2011.
The Boston Consulting Group (BCG) on behalf of the Global e-Sustainability Initiative (2012) *GeSI SMARTer 2020: The Role of ICT in Driving a Sustainable Future* (gesi.org/assets/js/lib/tinymce/jscripts/tiny_mce/plugins/ajaxfilemanager/uploaded/SMARTer%202020%20-%20The%20Role%20of%20ICT%20in%20Driving%20a%20Sustainable%20Future%20-%20December%202012.pdf).
www22.verizon.com/about/community/va/technology/tech_index.html

9
Combining social value with business opportunity
A 360-degree approach

How does a company promote leadership while also creating social value and opportunities for growth? The case of IBM provides a brilliant example of a company creating social value by building social capital, and examines how forging new relationships can lead to growth by leveraging the core competencies of IBM.

This chapter is based on classroom discussions and interviews from 2011 and 2012, and does not represent a totality of the activities in which the company is engaged. The diagram at the beginning of the chapter is meant to orient the reader as to the contents of the chapter rather than the breadth of issues covered by the company.

IBM

As IBM enters its second century, it possesses unique capabilities—in technology, in business expertise, and most importantly, in deep and systemic understanding of global citizenship—to lead the world in making that potential real... Business, in particular, must seize the initiative. We must not wait for government mandates. We must be active in convening all sectors of society to solve problems that none can solve on their own. We must energize our own resources—not just financial, but also human. Most crucially, we must create corporate citizenship and business strategies that are not merely "linked," but one.

Ginni Rometty, Chairman, President, and CEO, IBM

Background

Founded in Endicott, New York, in 1911, IBM manufactures and markets hardware and software; and offers infrastructure, hosting, and consulting services worldwide. IBM operates in 170 global markets and, with 434,246 employees, is the second largest firm in the United States. In 2012, the company recorded revenues of $104.5 billion with $16.6 billion in profits. The company has sought to become a **"globally integrated enterprise"** operating simultaneously as a global and a local company.[1]

The challenges of globalization

Among the challenges facing large multinational companies are globalization and how to develop leadership within a global context. In 2008, IBM had only a limited presence in emerging economies beyond the BRIC countries (Brazil, Russia, India, and China). How could IBM become relevant and visible in emerging countries such as Nigeria and Tanzania? Was there a way for IBM to gain an understanding of the challenges facing these countries and address the multi-faceted problems of these nations? How could IBM address the challenge of moving jobs overseas? What kinds of mechanisms exist for expanding business into emerging markets? The answers to these questions came from Kevin Thompson, a mid-level IBM employee, who had served in the Peace Corps. Why not create a Peace Corps within IBM to deploy teams of employees to address country challenges while helping promote leadership and team-building within IBM?

---

1 This term was coined by IBM Chief Executive Sam Palmisano in an article in *Foreign Affairs*, published in 2006. Quoted in IBM's "Corporate Service Corps: A New Model for Leadership Development, Market Expansion and Citizenship," IBM, 2011, p. 3.

Corporate Service Corps

To build a presence in emerging economies, IBM launched the Corporate Service Corps (CSC) in 2008 and then the Executive Service Corps (ESC) in 2010. The CSC sends teams of 8–15 IBM employees, known as IBMers, to emerging markets where they work with local government and business leaders to establish or improve new systems and processes. CSC teams include IBMers from around the globe, rather than one country or one division, which is crucial for perspective when teams are on-site. As of December 2012, the CSC had completed 120 projects in 25 countries from Chile to Ghana to Kazakhstan. More than 1,500 IBMers from around the globe participated in the program that has been referred to by many of them as, "life-altering."

The CSC delivers a 360-degree approach by providing a global service that benefits emerging markets, adds value to the company through employee training, and returns profits to IBM through the formation of profitable contracts. IBM's success in each of these areas through the CSC has changed how many people view the potential for corporate social responsibility (CSR). In fact, IBM has helped numerous companies establish similar programs.

Championing the CSC

Kevin Thompson, by his own admission, had no interest in business while he was growing up. As a Peace Corps alumnus, he had managed a tree farm in Ghana; he was trained as a scientist; and he hoped to play in a successful rock band. Kevin met his wife while pursuing a master's degree in horticulture and, while she finished her graduate degree, he "found his way" into business school at Cornell. He eventually secured a job with IBM in 2003 and, after a stint in strategy, Kevin found his niche in CSR.

While Kevin's background is not typical of a corporate executive working for a Dow Jones 100 company, he fully exemplifies many of the traditional characteristics of a successful executive. He is an

entrepreneur inside who is not afraid to take risks, and he is able to champion his ideas to propel them into reality.

Implementing the concept

When Kevin first approached his boss at IBM about the concept of a Peace Corps within the company, the response was less than enthusiastic. Kevin recalls, "the idea did face resistance.... It took many months before the program gained a profile and then several more months after that until it gained broader acceptance. Now, the company fully embraces the CSC as an embodiment of IBM's values." After the initial planning, Kevin and his team opened the application process to top-level performers in the company. Kevin commented that one senior executive thought they would be lucky to receive a few hundred applications. However, during the first application cycle, over 5,500 employees applied from 65 countries. The significant level of interest demonstrated the value of the CSC even before the project commenced.

CSC project team members are carefully selected depending on their specific areas of expertise. The program builds skills which not only advance their core work within IBM, but enhances their loyalty to IBM. The CSC is one of many assets that attract top talent to IBM.

A crucial way to make this type of work sustainable for a publicly traded corporation is to guarantee a tangible return on investment. IBM chooses projects in emerging markets where they can turn their charitable work into profitable contracts in the future.

One of IBM's best decisions was to partner with three organizations: CDC Development Solutions, Australian Business Partners, and Digital Opportunity Trust, all of whom specialize in international volunteer assignments. Kevin and his team recognized the value of hiring other companies to organize CSC projects and place volunteers.

The CSC has been described by alumni as a 30-day executive MBA course, with real-world experience replacing class time. Each CSC project requires six months of pre-work and three months of post-work. The actual trip lasts for one month, which Kevin and his team agreed was enough time to accomplish goals and not too much time away from the office. On assignment, team members must collaborate with one another, identify their strengths and weaknesses, and develop a solution together without assigning a leader. In many cases, the IBM teams build strong relationships with local leaders. These relationships have evolved into profitable contracts for IBM, allowing the company to return to these emerging economies to provide more project management and consulting services.

CSC in Nigeria

The five CSC projects implemented in Nigeria between 2009 and 2011 are an excellent representation of the 360-degree effect of the CSC. Four of the five projects were carried out in Calabar, the central city of Cross River State, over the course of a year. Among many initiatives, the first CSC project team developed a database for maternal and child resources as well as an enterprise architecture framework for the Cross River State government. "Nigeria is a critically important country for our business, and for the continent of Africa," Kevin said. "We were surprised about the business opportunity that developed from our Nigeria program. Calabar wasn't on the radar screen of our business teams." The CSC teams became closely acquainted with the Governor of Cross River State, Liyel Imoke, who is now one of the most influential leaders in Nigeria, the most populous country in Africa.

IBMers improved numerous IT systems that helped the government run more efficiently and developed lasting relationships with local leaders. Due to the strength of the relationship with Imoke, and his high opinion of IBM, the company landed its first service contract in West Africa worth $1.2 million. Imoke's vision was to expand the rural healthcare system that he had helped establish in Cross River State to the rest of Nigeria. As Kevin noted, this project encapsulates CSC's ability to create both leadership and societal value, while also propelling a local leader to prominence through his work and affiliation with IBM. The initial philanthropic project to help set up rural health clinics for mothers and small children led directly to a business deal.

CSC in Egypt

Egypt is an important country for IBM's business objectives as it is one the largest countries in Africa. CSC team members for the Egypt projects had backgrounds in technology, consulting, research, marketing, and finance. Eleven IBMers were sent to Luxor to improve the local conditions and create income-generating activities. The team collaborated mainly with the Egyptian Ministry of Trade and Industry as well as the Ministry of Agriculture. In addition, they worked with the Governor of Luxor and UNESCO.

The team focused on two projects. The first helped smallholder farmers maximize their income through the creation of additional income-generating opportunities. The second helped the Nubian population to preserve and promote their cultural heritage through recommendations for improving the sustainability of cultural projects. The team identified opportunities to connect with the wider Nubian community and market opportunities. They also recommended a business structure to create a crafts market, and invested in widening the market opportunities to share their heritage with surrounding communities. One of the highlights for the second CSC team in Luxor was creating a website for the Suzanne Mubarak Regional Centre for Women's Health and Development. The Centre seeks to improve women's health throughout Africa, the Middle East, and the Arab world. It provides training to healthcare professionals; conducts laboratory, clinical, and epidemiological research on matters related to women's health and development; and supports an extensive library of medical texts.

In collaboration with several agencies of the United Nations, another team conducted a complete supply chain mapping of key local horticultural crops. They identified gaps and provided recommendations which enabled smallholder farmers to improve their position in the supply chain. One recommendation was to expand agriculture to become the second leading economic sector in the Luxor region. In addition, they trained vocational school students in business skills.

CSC in Sichuan Province, China

When Jordan Olivero departed to the Sichuan Province in China shortly after they suffered an earthquake of magnitude 8.0, he had no idea what to expect from his CSC enrollment. What he found in Sichuan was a city badly damaged, but with extensive potential for growth. The team's mission on this trip was to provide objective advice on growing the infrastructure in Sichuan. Jordan worked with government officials, reviewing both the IT and logistics sectors, to identify backlogs and inefficiencies. IBMers worked with local businesses and the Sichuan Chamber of Commerce to build positive public relations with the city's residents.

Jordan described this experience as one of the most fundamental career-building opportunities of his life, as he learned invaluable skills about interacting and working with foreign clients. In the past, he stated that he was always myopically focused when completing a task, and often did not spend enough time developing relationships or building trust with clients. Working with the Chinese and learning the value they place on trust and relationships vastly improved his future client relationships.

Soon after his team left China, the Sichuan Chamber of Commerce contracted IBM to build systems to help streamline traffic activity in all areas, not just those affected by the earthquake. This exemplifies the effect of the CSC: they were able to assist a city in need, secure a business contract, and enhance the leadership skills of IBMers. Four years later, Jordan still looks back on this experience as one of the most pivotal moments of his professional career.

The Executive Service Corps (ESC)

An off-shoot of the CSC, the ESC sends IBM executives to emerging markets to work with high-level city and national officials. These IBMers have already established themselves as leaders in their own field, so ESC projects focus on more complex issues within countries deemed to have tremendous growth potential. The ESC project in Thailand included five IBMers from the United States, France, and the Netherlands. The team assisted two local organizations, Smarter Healthcare and Smarter Food, which focused on improving hospital efficiencies and creating a data resource center for farmers to share information, respectively. ESC teams are smaller than CSC teams, usually five or six people, but despite the strong leadership abilities they display in their permanent jobs, no one is allowed to take charge. Like the CSC, ESC team members must collaborate and determine solutions as a unit.

Building a smarter planet

Kevin affirmed that, until now, there have been clear lines between government, NGOs, for-profit corporations, and CSR. IBM has a program, "Building a Smarter Planet," that focuses on eliminating these lines with programs like the CSC. According to IBM's Chairman, President, and CEO, Ginni Rometty:

> *Building a Smarter Planet, it turns out, requires building a new kind of corporation. That will not happen overnight. But the game-changing progress described in this report gives me confidence that it is achievable. As we have for 100 years—and counting—IBMers, our partners, and the communities we serve are still, together, dedicated to making our world literally work better.*[2]

According to Kevin, "IBM is doing business by solving societal issues. Smarter Planet really is a study in systems thinking, and IBM is trying to elevate to this systems level view because... everything is connected."

2   "Letter from the President and CEO," in IBM Corporate Responsibility Report 2011 (www.ibm.com/ibm/responsibility/2011/bin/downloads/ IBM_Corp_Responsibility_Report_2011.pdf), p. 1.

The future of the CSC and CSR

Kevin believes that the lines between governments, NGOs, and for-profit corporations are blurring, and they will continue to blur as businesses continue to operate in a global environment. He calls this trend "**sector blur**." IBM now operates in spaces like water and traffic congestion, "problems that used to be the domains of government," said Kevin.

According to Kevin, the CSR movement will continue: "if you are doing something right, you do not need to over design or over engineer it." Just as human resources (HR), marketing, and social media, have become part of business operations, Kevin believes CSR, as we know it today, will become part of the basic license to operate for every business. Unlike marketing, CSR has struggled to define ways to measure its success within an organization. As he said, "Marketing established a seat in the C-suite. There is real academic work. There are measurements in marketing, you have a profession in marketing, and you can major in marketing, so marketing is here to stay for the foreseeable future." CSR is not yet established in the same ways as marketing and HR. Combined with growing transparency and better communication with customers thanks to Web 2.0 technology, CSR might become an important strategic executive position. However, it may also become incorporated into the everyday thinking of all employees.

Based on Kevin's prediction of the continued blurring of sectors, the role of CSR at IBM will continue to evolve. When asked about the future of the CSC, Kevin responded that the program is stable and is a core part of IBM's program portfolio. As he points out, IBM must find opportunities where movement is not only possible, but desirable. Working with IBM carries significant credibility and clout for leaders in developing countries, as it did for Liyel Imoke in Nigeria. IBM's continued success will depend largely on their innovative problem-solving approach; continued development of strong relationships with local leaders based on integrity; and the willingness of emerging markets to welcome IBMers into their environment.

Sources

IBM (2011) *IBM's Corporate Service Corps: A New Model for Leadership Development, Market Expansion and Citizenship* (www.ibm.com/ibm/responsibility/corporateservicecorps/pdf/IBM_Corporate_Service_Corps_Essay.pdf).

Presentation by Kevin Thompson, Manager, IBM Center for Applied Insights, Babson, December 4, 2012.

10

Serving new markets

The development of a new product or service can create social value. The story of BiddingForGood demonstrates how the sheer existence of a company can create social value and how entrepreneurs have an important role to play in driving change in society.

This chapter is based on classroom discussions and interviews from 2011 and 2012, and does not represent a totality of the activities in which the company is engaged. The diagram at the beginning of the chapter is meant to orient the reader as to the contents of the chapter rather than the breadth of issues covered by the company.

BiddingForGood

"A culture which supports social value creation requires participation from all ranks—it has to really be part of the culture of the company."

Jon Carson, CEO, BiddingForGood

Background

BiddingForGood (BFG) is an online auction house that aims to transform the silent auction fundraising platform for non-profits. BFG allows more people in more geographically diverse areas to participate in the bidding process, increasing the frequency and price of bids. This makes the auction a more lucrative fundraiser for the non-profit beneficiary and more engaging for participants. BFG also offers

for-profit organizations a free service to handle and streamline donation requests.

Strategies

The mission of BiddingForGood is to revolutionize silent auctions,
which it has successfully accomplished. BFG has removed some
of the inefficiencies of silent auctions, such as restricted audience
sizes, limits on simultaneous bids, the inability to prioritize between
different auction items, and the inability to track the bid status on
particular items. Product leadership (event sponsorships and a robust
donation and auction platform) along with customer service are the
two pillars of BFG's competitive advantage. Unlike eBay, BFG is a
specialist within its market, providing the advantage of focus.

BFG faces some challenges. In general, non-profits are late adopters
of technology, and using the Internet for fundraising is a difficult concept for first-timers. This has necessitated a dedicated sales team and
some hand-holding of non-profits through their first auction. Attracting customers was a real challenge in the beginning. However, focus
and continuous differentiation in the marketplace has enabled BFG to
cross the chasm from an outbound to an inbound sales model. 1,000
auctions were executed through BFG in the first four years, while the
next 1,000 auctions were completed within just 14 months. Today,
BFG executes 1,000 auctions every 90 days and receives 1,500 inquir-
ies per month.

Pricing of software, which is available on the Internet, is also a
tricky challenge as these are high-margin, yet scalable products.
BFG put considerable thought into pricing its offering, which it has
recently revised. At BFG, non-profits pay an annual membership fee
of $600. This fixed payment ensures that the non-profit is commit-
ted to using BFG for auctions ("skin in the game"). BFG experiences
a client attrition rate of 30% annually, which is primarily made up
of organizations who have less experience using an online auction
for the first time and, therefore less successful auctions. The annual

membership fee pricing model is a way to help reduce attrition by tying the organization to BFG for a longer time period, allowing for follow-on auction experiences.

BFG also charges the client a performance fee based on the total proceeds of the auction. Volume is rewarded; BFG takes a lower percentage of the revenues of larger auctions. (See Table 10.1.)

Table 10.1 **Performance fee calculations**

Source: Slide presentation from Jon Carson at Babson

Online auction item proceeds	BiddingForGood's performance fee
$0–20,000	9%
$20,001–50,000	6%
$50,001+	3%

Overall, BFG operates on an 83% gross margin and guarantees the non-profit at least 91% of the auction collections. On average, a non-profit makes $6 for every $1 they give BFG. At times, skeptics question whether BFG really "earned" the 9% from the non-profit. Under scrutiny is the question of "appropriate profitability" in social businesses.

Appropriate profitability

BiddingForGood's CEO, Jon Carson, confessed that this is an on-going challenge that every social business faces. BFG, according to Jon, provides a fair value proposition to its customers, which is why they continue to pay for the service. Jon also highlighted that their returns to non-profits (91%+) are significantly higher than the returns offered by any other company, and asked the MBA students to think about whether that justifies equitable profitability. He stated that the margin BFG operates on is necessary for survival, and asked if this sort of profitability was fair if it kept this service in business to support the non-profits.

Profitability is a significant concern in BFG's social engagement strategy. Operating a for-profit company that services non-profits requires care to ensure profit margins are reasonable relative to the service provided. While some may question the amount BFG returns to non-profits, the company does provide a larger market opportunity for non-profit organizations by expanding participation in auctions while simultaneously providing bargain deals for customers (items sell for on average 30% below retail). This revenue model allows the seller to add value to its investors and returns a greater profit than a localized auction. Had BFG not followed its mission and focused solely on profits over "good," this opportunity would likely have gone unnoticed. Instead, they have a tenable business plan that is more than just a marketing scheme.

In 2011, National Public Radio reported on companies that, at first glance, appeared to be charitable; but, in reality, are just using their charitable status to disingenuously drive profit. While BFG declined the opportunity to act as a counter-example, the story highlighted the fact that the public questions the integrity of companies and their reasons for being charitable. A disingenuous motive can tarnish a company's reputation and, ultimately, its profitability. Therefore, finding the balance between fiduciary responsibility to investors and reasonable pricing structures for charitable organizations is a difficult, but essential task for BFG. Ensuring that the company's value proposition creates a win-win is imperative. The fact that it took four years to host the first 1,000 auctions and now only three months to do so, indicates a compelling value proposition which is increasing in strength. However, remaining genuine and honest in pricing structures will be essential to the long-term success of BFG, both for the social value creation initiatives and for the company as a whole.

Leadership

The story of how Jon Carson came to BiddingForGood is compelling and provides some unexpected lessons. Often, social entrepreneurs start from the identification of a social problem and a desire to improve their community. Students expected that Jon started BFG from an altruistic standpoint, with the mission of doing "good." Jon is a serial entrepreneur; BFG is his fourth company and he began with a more simplistic, market-driven viewpoint.

After selling his previous company, Family Education Network, Jon spent time exploring potential next steps for his career. During this time, he was introduced to the founder of BFG and recognized the opportunity to create a viable, venture-backed business plan. For Jon, there were several key components that led him to pursue this social venture (and that he believes are essential to any company desiring venture funding):

- There was a large sandbox to play in: the fundraising auction market was estimated to be worth $16 billion annually, and there were 1.9 million non-profits looking for funding. He recognized that he could create a huge business even by attracting a small portion of the market.

- The company had been building momentum, even without a good management process in place.

- BFG had a believable business model that had been proven elsewhere (e.g., eBay).

- There was an opportunity to address a niche market that most other players in the field were not addressing appropriately. In this case, it was services for the non-profit marketplace.

Social value creation in and through BiddingForGood

BiddingForGood did not start with a focus on creating social value. The original founder was focused on generating profits in order to move the company towards an initial public offering (IPO). Similarly, many of BFG's early hires shared a profit-centric view of the company. One of BFG's board members was, and still is, adamant that

Jon should not care about social value creation and should simply focus on the bottom line. Although BFG is a socially oriented organization, the realities of for-profit investments still apply. Moving away from this profit-only mentality has taken a mix of leadership from Jon and the employees.

After Jon took over at BFG, it was a grassroots effort that fostered a sense of social responsibility within the company. He said that, while he supports social objectives, the impetus for change boiled up from the bottom and permeated the organization with only minimal nurturing from him. Supporting small events, such as food drives and recycling, has enabled BFG's employees to express their commitment to "doing good." As Jon indicated, most people who come to work for BFG are already inclined towards doing good, they just need support to do it. Jon suggests that BFG's true identity is now starting to be expressed and, as a result, they are more successful in attracting people aligned with their "doing good" culture. However, he also argued that for this stance to really take hold at BFG, it needed support from Jon and the company's leadership. In Jon's words, "the CEO has to drink the Kool-Aid" for the mission to really take hold. Part of that leadership movement required that he let go of several employees who "just didn't get it."

A culture which supports social value creation requires participation from all ranks of the company. Corporate engagement is most effective when it is tied to both the culture and strategy of the organization. BFG is starting to engage employees more fully and have a demonstrable positive effect on the community. (Its Good-o-Meter, which it is pushing other companies to adopt, shows the company has provided over $136 million to non-profits to date.)

Challenges and the future of BiddingForGood

BiddingForGood has grown substantially over the past nine years. However, the recession and several exciting new initiatives will change how BiddingForGood grows in the future. The growth of the

Internet and web-enabled devices provides exciting opportunities for non-profits, and BFG is focused on acting as a bridge to connect these technologies and organizations.

Like many companies in the U.S., the economic downturn has affected BFG. The recession created an overall reduction in donations, including strong erosion in the efficacy of traditional silent auctions. Non-profits that used to host their own silent auctions have found challenges in raising money through this medium as people have not been spending or donating as much. This dilemma has led many organizations to turn to BFG to replace this lost revenue stream. In this way, the recession has had a positive effect on BFG; however, the effect of layoffs across the country has had the opposite effect. In a number of organizations, the primary person who runs auctions (BFG's key contact) has been fired, while the number of items donated to auctions has also decreased. Jon worries about these factors as well as the future of spending following the economic downturn. He claims it has not yet affected his business, but anticipates that it will. The economy has affected every business in one way or another, and a business rooted in social entrepreneurship is no different.

To get ahead of these hard times, Jon and BFG are designing a way to auction items on a phone or any mobile device. "Everyone has a mobile device," says Jon. BFG is in the process of trying to find better solutions to a few problems with this new platform, such as registration, placing the first bid, and checkout. The logic is that this new way to run auctions will create an even larger bidding pool, more competition in auctions, and greater final bid amounts. With the mobile application, the auction market for non-profits should be substantially large, thereby bringing more clients to BFG and creating a benefit for both the non-profits and the company.

BFG also has a plan for improving their services from a social perspective. One platform Jon has recently designed helps for-profit corporations manage their constant barrage of sponsorship requests from non-profits. This not only right-sizes auctions and giving, but also gives BFG a huge database of non-profits asking for help. BFG is hoping that, in a few years, this information and knowledge will create another revenue stream through expanding their social benefits to non-profit fundraisers (and the for-profits supporting them).

This plan emphasizes an important point about BFG: the company's bottom line is always considered when moving forward with an initiative. While BFG tries to ensure that their efforts will help non-profits as much as possible, they are very cognizant of their return on investment. While the fundamental mission of Jon and the business is social, like many other companies across various industries, what they choose to do has to help BFG and its shareholders as well. These new initiatives are good steps that will help BFG fight the difficulties of the recent recession while simultaneously increasing opportunities for their non-profit customers and for themselves.

BFG is working to position itself as an end-to-end event management platform for auction fundraisers. The company realized that its clients are running events involving other economic activities, such as tickets, raffles, live gavel auctions, close-outs, and payment processing. According to Jon, there are a number of emerging event management companies commanding billion-dollar valuations which lack a philanthropic presence.

Questions from students for Jon Carson, CEO of BiddingForGood

Q: How did you develop the pricing strategy?

A: We entered into the space of an 800 pound gorilla (eBay) and found an area where eBay was not active. The charity auction space was not big enough to be of interest to eBay. We looked at all of the inefficiencies of silent auctions for charities and saw how technology could address the inefficiencies. For example, before BFG, only people in the room could bid as there were barriers of time and geography. There were crowds to fight once you found items to bid on. It is impossible to be at four clipboards at once.

We also knew that charities are risk-averse and need some hand-holding. The customers need good customer service to explain the model and reassure them. eBay is very much self-service.

We also looked at how we could aggregate the market, which is generally staffed by volunteers. This is a very complicated market.

We struggled with pricing. We needed to have a fixed fee of $600 to make sure the clients had skin in the game. We also look at how to be more and more attractive to bigger clients. We want to reward value.

We charge more than eBay, but we are still in conformance with the Better Business Bureau Guidelines. If we are not commercially viable, we cannot help non-profits to grow.

Q: What major changes do you see to the business model?

A: All business models rest on three legs: acquisition, yield, and retention. Our challenge has been around acquisition. It took time and money, but we solved this through scale. This market is highly fragmented, as each auction is only in the market for 90 days. We needed to look at how the market aggregates.

Our approach was to go to the manager of the Liberty Hotel and to build a system for them to manage all of the requests from charities. We now have a tool that hotels, restaurants, and others can use when items are requested for charity auctions. When the Hotel gets a request, the system generates an email that goes out to the charity. The tool is free for the first year and then companies pay $200 after.

Q: To what extent are you a social entrepreneur? How do you balance social concerns with profitability?

A: There are definitional issues around social entrepreneurship. What is it? Who is a social entrepreneur? The concept emanates from the belief system of the founder. Is the company anchored in having some tangible ways of making the world better? BFG has a social mission.

There is a tension in terms of CSR, as our goal is to hire the best people, but they may not have a serious commitment to social issues. We encourage employees to volunteer.

Q: How will BFG manage in a time of economic downturn?

A: Non-profits are cutting their budgets. For example, the Boston Food Bank has cut staff. This means that they may have more of a need for our services. We need to find ways to remotely support charity events. Charitable giving is decreasing, but e-commerce is on the rise.

We also know that 60% of non-profits are experiencing a surge in demand for their services and will need to find alternate funding as government budgets are cut.

Source

Presentation by Jon Carson, CEO, BiddingForGood, Babson, December 13, 2011.

11
Leadership and social value creation

Social value creation is about transformation, and leadership is a key part of that process. This chapter examines what it takes to provide leadership to create social value and manage complexity, while developing sustainability systems.

This chapter is based on classroom discussions and interviews from 2011 and 2012, and does not represent a totality of the activities in which the company is engaged. The diagram at the beginning of the chapter is meant to orient the reader as to the contents of the chapter rather than the breadth of issues covered by the company.

UPS

What does it take to drive change within a company?

Being a change agent within a corporation requires special skills and attributes that can foster an environment that creates social value. For 16 years, Lynnette McIntire has been a change agent within UPS, where she manages sustainability communications. She joined the company in 1997 as a member of the supply chain business unit, and has edited the company's sustainability report for four years. Lynnette is an **entrepreneur inside**, and her career inside UPS provides many useful lessons on navigating change.

Lynnette played a pivotal role in creating a culture of sustainability within UPS, and her success is due to her ability to play several roles within the company. Over the course of her career, Lynnette has been a translator, **influencer**, and storyteller.

Translator

When Lynnette joined UPS in 1997, the company did not yet have a culture of sustainability and lacked systems to address social and environmental concerns. When asked what she is most proud of in her 16-year career at UPS, Lynnette responded that developing a **materiality matrix** was among her crowning achievements. Lynnette worked with Business for Social Responsibility (BSR) to understand the sustainability issues that are important to customers, investors, employees, and civil society. Stakeholders identified 166 issues that are material to UPS. The **materiality matrix** provides a language that allowed UPS to translate stakeholder concerns into internal policy, and is guiding the company's future sustainability initiatives.

Table 1 **Materiality matrix**

www.responsibility.ups.com/community/Static%20Files/sustainability/2011_UPS_CSR_Report.pdf

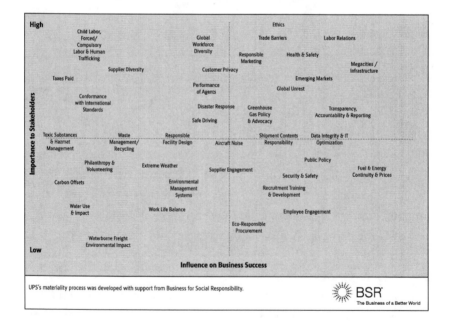

Influencer

In order to create social value, leaders like Lynnette galvanize employees to be part of the change within the organization. Lynnette was an **influencer** within UPS, spearheading a program to create Sustainability Ambassadors within the company. Over 1,400 employees in many different countries where UPS operates have signed up to the program. **Influencers** enlist other change agents, creating a multiplier effect.

Storyteller

Lynnette is a brilliant storyteller. In her Southern accent, she tells her story and the story of the company that she has helped to transform. To drive change within UPS, she enlisted people and influenced others, largely through her ability to tell stories that resonate with stakeholders. Nate Garvis, a Senior Fellow in Social Innovation at Babson and author of the book *Naked Civics*, uses the term **80% storyteller** to describe a special talent of storytellers to tell 80% of the story, leaving 20% up to the listener to fill in the contours. In this way, **influencers** like Lynnette are able to draw in others, engaging them in creating part of the story. Lynnette has been an **80% storyteller**, encouraging employees to add their own dimensions to the evolving narrative.

What are the competencies needed to drive change?

As mentioned in Chapter 4, the Boston College Center for Corporate Citizenship, in coordination with the Hay Group, developed a model identifying eight key competencies for success in corporate citizenship. As a rapidly changing discipline with a unique set of challenges, the study was established to answer the question: "Where do corporate citizen leaders come from?" The Leadership Competencies for Corporate Citizenship report that emerged was based on focus groups conducted with successful leaders in corporate social responsibility (CSR) to uncover their common skills and personality traits. What followed was the identification of eight key factors, balanced between internal and external stimuli, which contributed to consistent success.

Lynnette has demonstrated her expertise in each of the model's eight competencies and serves as an example of effective leadership in action.

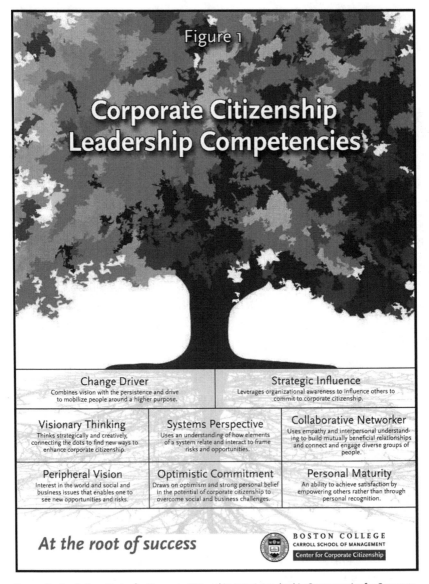

Figure 1

Corporate Citizenship Leadership Competencies

Change Driver
Combines vision with the persistence and drive to mobilize people around a higher purpose.

Strategic Influence
Leverages organizational awareness to influence others to commit to corporate citizenship.

Visionary Thinking
Thinks strategically and creatively, connecting the dots to find new ways to enhance corporate citizenship.

Systems Perspective
Uses an understanding of how elements of a system relate and interact to frame risks and opportunities.

Collaborative Networker
Uses empathy and interpersonal understanding to build mutually beneficial relationships and connect and engage diverse groups of people.

Peripheral Vision
Interest in the world and social and business issues that enables one to see new opportunities and risks.

Optimistic Commitment
Draws on optimism and strong personal belief in the potential of corporate citizenship to overcome social and business challenges.

Personal Maturity
An ability to achieve satisfaction by empowering others rather than through personal recognition.

At the root of success

BOSTON COLLEGE
CARROLL SCHOOL OF MANAGEMENT
Center for Corporate Citizenship

Source: Boston College Center for Corporate Citizenship (2010), *Leadership Competencies for Corporate Citizenship: Getting to the roots of success* (Boston College Center for Corporate Citizenship, www.BCCorporateCitizenship.org).

Peripheral vision

A general awareness of external factors that could contribute to or hinder organizational success, and interest in discovering new trends, risks, and current events. Commitment to avoiding tunnel vision in order to prevent surprises, and remain agile in adapting a strategy. Can articulate to management what others outside the organization think about current practices (or popular practices within the industry) and explain why that is important.

Throughout her tenure at UPS, Lynnette has applied her natural inquisitiveness and analytical ability to champion new initiatives at the company. She developed these skills early on, well before joining the company.

After graduating from the University of Minnesota, Minneapolis, with a bachelor's degree in Journalism, Lynnette joined the staff of her hometown newspaper in Kentucky. Later, she moved to *The Memphis Commercial Appeal*'s Greenville, Mississippi, bureau. There, she covered local business news across the Mississippi Delta region, and found herself responsible for identifying, writing, and submitting five articles per day. She pinpoints this as her first introduction to entrepreneurial thinking. As these stories were clearly not going to find her, Lynnette had to motivate herself to seek them out on her own.

Eventually, she transitioned her communication skills over to the world of public relations, accepting a position at a firm in Minnesota. It was here that she got her introduction to the world of operational logistics and distribution. FedEx was one of her company's largest clients, and in order to effectively represent them, Lynnette had to gain an understanding of the unique financial and strategic characteristics of the company. Her success in the position, and a job with the global agency Shandwick, led to an assignment in Bangkok, Thailand, where she worked alongside the founder of the first public relations firm in the country.

The early 1990s were a time of great economic and social change in Bangkok, with an emerging middle-class creating a wealth of opportunity for multinational corporations to enter the market. Lynnette worked with companies such as Procter & Gamble and Northwest Airlines to introduce new product innovations to Southeast Asia. After five years overseas, including a stint with FedEx establishing their communications program in Asia, she moved back to the United States to continue in public relations for several years before moving to UPS to join their new supply chain solutions business unit.

These early experiences undoubtedly contributed to Lynnette's ability to thrive in environments that are continuously evolving. Whether she was in the field as a journalist looking for her next story or working in an emerging economy, the start of her career was defined by her ability to find her bearings in unknowable situations. Interacting with the world at large and gaining exposure to multiple industries provided Lynnette with the skills that allowed her to understand the big picture, and to understand how UPS's corporate citizenship policies affected stakeholders outside of the organization as well as inside.

Visionary thinking

Leaders with this skill can visualize the connections that exist between corporate citizenship and all other areas of the business. They understand that both can exist at the same time and can in fact be drivers of success for each other.

Lynnette was assigned as Director of Global Reputation Management, and her expertise in public relations combined with her position on the supply chain team made her an obvious choice to lead the charge on the company's sustainability efforts. One of her first assignments was to assess the company's global reputation. As the eighth largest airline in the world and one of the world's largest transportation companies, fuel and environmental concerns could be major reputation risks. On the opportunity side, UPS had nearly a century's worth of goodwill generated through philanthropy, employee volunteerism, and a leadership position in community service. The company had produced its first sustainability report in 2002, one of the earliest in the United States, but little had been done by the company to keep up with the growing expectations and standards that were emerging around sustainability. The evidence was that UPS's rankings and grades were slipping on surveys, external research reports, and rankings. In some cases, UPS had dropped from As to Cs or even Ds.

Lynnette joined a small group of sustainability advocates from across the company to re-invigorate UPS's sustainability leadership. One of those advocates was Kurt Kuehn, the company's current Chief Financial Officer (appointed in 2008). Kurt joined UPS in 1977 as a driver and moved his way up the ranks to an executive management position, taking on roles in sales and marketing, strategic cost planning, and engineering along the way. Kurt was an early supporter of the company's sustainability initiatives, including supporting the first UPS sustainability report when he was the head of UPS's Investor Relations group. Kurt, along with Bob Stoffel, who had led the supply chain business unit, sponsored the creation of a new governance system for sustainability that included a steering committee of senior management; a working committee for front-line managers involved in sustainability-related projects; and a newly created sustainability team for data collection and program development. Lynnette created that first structure that still exists today.

The development of the report reflects the visionary thinking of both Lynnette and Kurt who recognized the value it would add to the company. While it is admirable for a company to devote time, energy, and money to creating social and environmental programs, without a system for tracking, analyzing, and communicating those efforts, they will likely stagnate and go unnoticed. As of 2011, the UPS Corporate Responsibility Report spanned a mammoth 165 pages, complete with seven appendices, and provided insight into the company's global operations. The Report earned an A+ Application Level by the Global Reporting Initiative, signifying superior transparency, and continues to serve as a leading example of effectiveness.

Systems perspective

An appreciation of how interrelated systems act in coordination to provide a framework for projects and opportunities. This allows the leader to identify and address concerns that apply to individual stake-holders by assessing the risks created by a new process. Individuals who possess this quality are able to effectively communicate these viewpoints to key decision-makers in their company.

By 2009, UPS was making great strides in improving their sustainability efforts and reporting methods. However, there was one key stakeholder whose voice was eager to be incorporated into the process: the customer. As customers became more informed about concerns relating to climate change and pollution, they began to demand solutions for the environmental toll that shipping took on the planet. In response to this outcry, Lynnette worked with UPS to introduce the first carbon-neutral shipping option of its kind. Customers who wished to participate had the option of accepting a small additional charge (5–25 cents) to their shipping order, which allowed UPS to buy a carbon offset on their behalf based on the actual carbon produced by their shipment. The program launched in October 2009 for domestic shipping and expanded to international operations in 2010. The funds generated are kept in a separate UPS account that is only used for supporting the program. In other words, the company does not profit at all from these fees.

As of 2011, 50,000 customers had participated in the program, which contributes to worldwide projects designed to reduce harmful gasses, replant forests, and sustainably treat wastewater. Surprisingly, executive management agreed to the new initiative without demanding a case for return on investment. They simply wanted to satisfy a demand of their customers. Lynnette's ability to recognize the importance of viewpoints that existed outside her company's doors demonstrates her understanding of systems perspectives. She was able to work with others to communicate the need for a new product and design a solution, effectively creating a win-win situation for both the consumer and the company.

Optimistic commitment

Committed to the belief that corporate citizenship will add value to their organization. This allows them to keep going regardless of

setbacks and opposition. Demonstrates interest in social value crea-
tion outside of their company, unafraid to take on big projects and
make adjustments along the way, proud of progress made.

UPS has a long history of contributing to the community, largely
driven by The UPS Foundation, which was founded in 1951. As a
leader in logistics planning, the company often volunteers its services to provide free consulting to food banks and humanitarian relief
efforts in order to increase effectiveness. With IT integration contributing largely to the company's success, employees are allowed to
work around the world to assist smaller organizations with technology solutions and business planning. It also provides in-kind shipping
for humanitarian and disaster relief.

However, one of the most unique features of UPS's corporate out-
reach is the company's Community Internship Program. Originally
founded in 1968 as a way to provide sensitivity training to trouble-
some employees, the program has flourished with staff members eager
to take part. Teams are sent to one of four locations: New York City;
Chattanooga, Tennessee; San Francisco; and McAllen, Texas, a border
town in the Rio Grande Valley. Each group of employees are charged
with solving social problems unique to that area by utilizing their business skills and a limited budget. While the company certainly benefits
from the leadership development and positive press generated by the
program, the effects go much deeper. Manager participants gain an
understanding of the wider world outside of corporate management,
and gain insights about the challenges facing hourly employees who
represent a large portion of the company's work force. Lynnette was
a participant in the McAllen program and speaks regularly to other
employee groups about the insights she gained.

Lynnette demonstrates her optimistic commitment to corporate citizenship through her continued efforts to drive initiatives at UPS. But
it is often difficult for workers who do not regularly engage in social
value creation to gain awareness of how wide-ranging the effects of
a well-run corporate citizenship program can be. The Community
Internship Program allows participants to experience that value first-
hand, and bring that knowledge back to their positions throughout

the organization. Through this experience, UPS is training its staff members in optimistic commitment and strengthening its business as a result.

Strategic influence

Inspires those around them to become involved in corporate citizenship efforts. This competency relates to an individual's communication skills and ability to influence stakeholders who they do not hold authoritative power over.

As a trained journalist with years of experience in the public relations world, Lynnette already possessed excellent communication skills by the time she joined the team at UPS. However, she found herself having to adapt to new styles early on to successfully partner with departments outside of the supply chain division. When she joined UPS, the company was undergoing a series of 45 mergers and acquisitions, and was quickly gaining market share. While this rapid growth was instrumental in the organization's rise as an industry leader, the company also experienced the typical growing pains that result from such a strategy. Forty-five new mergers meant that hundreds of new employees joined the company, coming from dozens of different office cultures and approaches to delivery service. Lynnette was faced with the challenge of finding common ground with many of these new divisions to successfully reach her department's goals. Even more importantly, she had to introduce the new services of a logistics unit to the parent company which largely saw itself as only a small package delivery company.

Lynnette tapped into her diverse background to effectively convey her message. She sought ways to explain her business unit's operations in a relatable manner, rather than attempt to "educate" them on the technical intricacies that were less important. On the surface, supply chain logistics may appear to be a complicated process—particularly at one of the largest delivery services in the world. However, at its core, the method is simply a progression of common sense steps. Lynnette recognized this and was able to explain her division's operations to co-workers by comparing them to those of another company that everyone was familiar with: the supply chain of Starbucks. Her experience as a journalist and public relations professional prepared her well for taking a complicated subject and breaking it into digestible parts. Her approach allowed her to build strong partnerships across the corporation and build on her network of stakeholders.

Change driver

Influences others in a way that draws different stakeholders together to work towards a common goal. When combined with skills in systems perspective, an individual can effectively introduce long-lasting corporate citizenship policies into many areas of a company. Activities that contribute to success in this competency include establishing regulated policies, setting goals, and tracking progress. This ability is closely related to possessing strategic influence, with a greater focus on the intellectual qualities that contribute to success.

While effectively communicating the importance of her role in layman's terms was one critical aspect of her job, Lynnette also quickly learned that it was equally valuable to demonstrate that she could articulate concepts to colleagues using business language. Her experience in business reporting and public relations meant that she understood the buzzwords and models, but it still took a conscious effort to adapt her way of thinking to this new context. Engineers and long-time transportation managers think and talk differently from communications professionals. However, once she identified this as a key factor of success, Lynnette's influence took off. Using charts, graphs, footnotes, and sources added legitimacy to her recommendations. Identifying strategies employed by UPS's competitors as a tool for benchmarking their own progress created a sense of urgency in improving their own processes. And conveying feedback that her department received from customers proved itself to be one of the most important strategies for presenting her case.

Combining her strategic influence with her role as a change driver led to the creation of a company-wide working committee, sourced from multiple departments which worked together to develop and implement sustainable initiatives. One of Lynnette's most valuable assets was the addition of what she calls her "Guardian Executives" to the team. Involving members of senior management who were highly invested in the committee's activities, with a level of decision-making power that allowed them to champion the team's goals, allowed for faster implementation and added legitimacy to the efforts.

Personal maturity

Empowering others in their organization to achieve a greater goal, rather than seeking recognition for themselves. Emotional intelligence increases the likelihood that their company will achieve more, because effort has been made to make lots of people feel connected to the mission. Comes down to affecting change, which can be difficult to champion.

Lynnette was surprised by the enthusiasm for her efforts that was displayed by some of the less obvious employees of the company. As a delivery company, UPS is one of the leading consumers of fossil fuels, and Lynnette's team is always on the lookout for ways to reduce consumption. In the wake of increased sustainability communications, the organization's automotive team developed a company-wide marketing effort to raise awareness of the issue by designing a mascot, "Mr. Fuel Drop." The initiative was a great success, and relates back to the value of communicating issues in relatable terms. The campaign took on a life of its own, with new characters and situations introduced to Mr. Fuel Drop along the way. If Lynnette had not worked to include all divisions of the company into her work, she could have missed out on learning about this valuable engagement tool.

Collaborative networker

The ability to listen to others and incorporate their needs and opinions into company goals and projects, even those who criticize. Brings people together by communicating what different groups need or have in common. Willingness to create cross-departmental partnerships and become a valued member of those teams, and to communicate mutually beneficial outcomes for all parties.

When asked to identify the accomplishments she is most proud of, Lynnette spoke of the value of her team of sustainability ambassadors. These volunteers come from a wide array of departments and work to communicate the importance of promoting social and environmental efforts. The excitement and dedication that the staff shows towards these efforts is a far cry from when Lynnette first sat down to re-ignite the company's commitment to sustainability. By encouraging communication between as many departments as possible, UPS is able to identify partnerships and streamline processes. Although much of the organization's success is due to the high level of staff engagement, that would not have been possible without Lynnette's skills at connecting people and communicating effectively.

Sources

This chapter is based on an interview between Lynnette McIntire and Cheryl Kiser, Deborah Leipziger, Emily Weiner, and Ana-Lisa Jones, April 21, 2013.

UPS (United Parcel Service) (2011) "UPS Sustainability Report."

UPS (United Parcel Service) (2011) "Corporate Sustainability Report: Logistics at the core," www.responsibility.ups.com/community/Static%20Files/sustainability/2011_UPS_CSR_Report.pdf, August 2013.

Max 19th Annual Awards: The Marketing Award for Excellence (2011) www.robinson.gsu.edu/resources2/files/marketing/maxawards/2011/about_ups_carbon.html.

www.ups.com/pressroom/us/bios/bios/About+UPS/UPS+Leadership/Speeches/Kurt+Kuehn/ci.Kurt+Kuehn.syndication

Concluding thoughts

When I thought about designing an intellectual and emotional journey for our students around the notion of Creating Social Value, I had the traditional MBA student in mind for a very simple reason. For over 15 years, I had the privilege of working with business leaders from around the world on creating strategies, management practices, and operations that aligned Corporate Social Responsibility to core business strategy. As a director at the Boston College Center for Corporate Citizenship, I regularly thought that someday business leaders would know that, from day one, they would be able to design a new set of values into their products and services. Social value.

At the Boston College Center, we worked with seasoned business leaders. But, what if we could start shaping the experience of young business leaders early on in their MBA education? Why wait for this crucial, yet complex journey to begin? After all, today more than ever, Social Value Creation is as essential to business as any other function like marketing, finance, HR, operations, etc.

If you have read any part of this book, you have entered into an important conversation that we will continue here at Babson College. We will continue to bring in companies, we will continue to encourage our students to be actively curious and committed to creating social value, and we will continue to share these conversations with you through our website. We are willing to share our journey as a school because we are dedicated to creating entrepreneurial leaders inside and outside large organizations. We encourage our students to take very seriously the notion of creating economic and social value everywhere, and most importantly, simultaneously not sequentially.

The authors of this book, the students who participated in the Social Value Creation Matters course, and the business leaders who committed their time to be profiled in this book all hope that you will experiment with being positive disruptors. We encourage you to practice being entrepreneurs inside and design cultures of entrepre-neuring that have social value at their heart. In this way, you can help demonstrate that creating social value is not a siloed activity within a CSR department, but an integral part of business in today's global economy.

So, the question we leave you with is not what are you going to do, rather, what are you going to do NEXT?

Cheryl

To join the journey, visit www.CreatingSocialValueBook.com

Index